"A timely and important book ~~that will help~~ ... more naturally and effectively through connecting their friends to the gospel message."

GAVIN CALVER, CEO, Evangelical Alliance

"One of the most gratifying trends today is the revitalization of Christian apologetics. Not all is good, of course. But the present volume is more than good: it is superb. This wonderful book is as 'magnetic' as its title. Daniel Strange appeals to us from an astonishing variety of sources: popular culture, world religions, social trends and, of course, the Holy Bible. He never does this boastfully but is always sympathetic and persuasive. Required reading for anyone wanting to know the credibility of the Christian faith in a confusing time."

WILLIAM EDGAR, Professor of Apologetics, Westminster Theological Seminary, Philadelphia

"Dan Strange is 'convinced that the church has the opportunity to fill a massive gap in our secular and fragmented market'. Which is why he has given us this perceptive and somewhat unusual book. Using Bavinck, Scripture and an excellent knowledge of contemporary culture, he shows us how we can fill that gap by being magnets for the gospel. The more I read, the more I was drawn to this idea. We have someone wonderful to communicate—but sometimes we struggle to join the dots and make the connections with those around us. If that's you, then you will find this wee book a stimulating and refreshing guide."

DAVID ROBERTSON, Director, ASK, Sydney

"How can we reach people who think we're from another planet? This problematic feeling of disconnectedness in evangelism is addressed biblically, wisely and practically by Dr. Strange in *Making Faith Magnetic*. But he not only gives you helpful direction; he also encourages you in this important work of evangelism, as well. I highly recommend this."

TONY MERIDA, Pastor for Preaching and Vision, Imago Dei Church, Raleigh, North Carolina; Author, *Love Your Church*

"Building on the success of his first book, *Plugged In*, Dr Daniel Strange provides us not only with a model for evangelism and engagement but shows how Jesus—the way, the truth and the life—answers the fundamental questions, or magnetic points, that all human beings ask. In so doing, this book empowers Christians to engage with people and culture."

NOLA LEACH, CEO, Care

"Interesting, insightful and inspiring. This is a book that addresses the pressing questions and issues every human person struggles with and must face. And, it points us to the answer to them all! Check it out and see if I am right!"

DANIEL L. AKIN, President, Southeastern Baptist Theological Seminary

"This is one of the best books on evangelism: profound and perceptive and, above all, wonderfully fresh. Anyone who seeks to do evangelism will find tremendous insights here on the different ways in which God's good news connects to the lives of those around us. A book to read and reread!"

J.JOHN, Evangelist

"The best missional material not only informs the head but also transforms the heart and life of the reader. This is one of those books. A must-read for ANYONE with a desire to effectively reach others with the gospel. This is being added to our training curriculum with thanksgiving. It is as incisive as it is insightful— with a clear applicational paradigm for both the Christian in the workplace and the preacher in the pulpit—while remaining totally accessible and down to earth."

EFREM BUCKLE, Deputy CEO and Director of Training and Mentoring, London City Mission

"This is a needed resource for the church today. Daniel Strange helps us to reorient our approach to apologetics in this modern society, but does so in a way that doesn't compromise the good news of the gospel message."

JASON THACKER, Chair of Research in Technology Ethics, ERLC

DANIEL STRANGE

Making
Faith
Magnetic

Five Hidden
Themes Our Culture
Can't Stop Talking
About...

And How to
Connect Them
to Christ

Making Faith Magnetic
© Daniel Strange, 2021

Published by:
The Good Book Company

thegoodbook.com | thegoodbook.co.uk
thegoodbook.com.au | thegoodbook.co.nz | thegoodbook.co.in

ISBN: 9781784986506 | Printed in Turkey

Cover design by Faceout Studio, Molly von Borstel
Design and art direction by André Parker

Contents

Foreword
By Timothy Keller

Dan Strange has written another terrific, down-to-earth book to help believers engage in fruitful conversations with friends about faith.

In an earlier book, *Plugged In*, Dan outlines a way to "enter" another person's framework of beliefs about life, then to "explore" and "expose"—that is, to both affirm and yet challenge them—and finally to redirect their good aspirations away from idols toward Christ himself. This approach, called "subversive fulfillment," is the essence of good apologetics in a post-Christian, post-modern society.

In the present book, Dan briefly recaps the "subversive fulfillment" method, but his burden here is to show how this approach plays out specifically in five areas of human longing and need. Using the work of J.H. Bavinck, he argues that there are five fundamental things for which all human beings are searching and to which all of us are inevitably drawn "magnetically". They are totality (a way to fit into a larger whole), norm (a way to live a moral and good human life), deliverance (a way to fulfill and fix our incomplete hearts), destiny (a sense of freedom and agency in the world), and higher power (a way to know transcendence and the sacred).

While Bavinck the missionary applied these "magnetic points" to the world religions, Dan helps us apply them to secular people, but that presents a challenge.

As he notes in passing, some have wondered if secularism eliminates these magnetic points. After all, the agnostic or atheist does not believe in any higher power. And in key ways secular culture resists the other four points as well. It tells us to not find our identity by "fitting in" but by looking inside and defining ourselves. It tells us there are no true "norms" or moral absolutes for human life. It insists that we don't need anything to "fix" us—that we can fix and fulfill ourselves through self-realization. And it asserts that we are already free to live any way we want as long as we do not harm anyone. In all these ways secularism seems to refuse to pose the questions that the religions of the world are answering.

But in this case appearances are highly deceiving. With their "heads" secular people declare that there is no larger spiritual whole to fit into or transcendent realm to contact—that there are no moral absolutes, inner "God-shaped" empty spaces, or divine plans. Yet Dan shows that the ways secular people live, speak, and struggle reveal that they know better in their hearts. They are seeking these things—indeed they are assuming their existence—despite their protestations to the contrary.

To make this case to a secular friend requires great patience, gentleness and love, and a lot of time. But in each area Dan gives readers many cultural examples of these secular-yet-spiritual aspirations that will resonate. He provides tons of pointers on how to tease out and make visible the operation of these magnetic points in our lives.

Finally Dan turns to how Jesus fulfills each of these universal human longings in ways no other world religion can match.

Jesus gives us an identity that connects us rather than isolating us. He is the only one who can provide a moral norm (his own character) that doesn't descend into moralism. He alone brings a finished, accomplished deliverance rather than one we must perform for ourselves. He is the one thing you can live for that does not enslave but actually liberates you.

And he is the Higher Power, the High and Holy One—who became a human being we can know and love personally.

This little book edified me. It made me keep asking: "How shall we escape if we neglect so great a salvation?" (Hebrews 2 v 3, ESV).

Thanks to Dan Strange for writing this! Read it to appreciate your own salvation and in order to better recommend it to those you love.

Timothy Keller
Redeemer City to City

1. The Way Ahead

"You're on another planet."

If I were to say that to you, I doubt you'd take it as a compliment (or, for that matter, as a great way to invite someone to continue reading a book!). It's a common figure of speech that gives the impression of being disconnected, of not being in touch with reality.

And yet, for many Christians, that's how we increasingly feel. We sense that our Christian faith is disconnected from the lives of those around us who don't know Jesus. Our way of looking at the world feels a million miles away from theirs. We're afraid that were we to say what we're *really* thinking—or when we open our mouths and try—we'd get some very weird looks: *You're on another planet.* At the same time we might feel this same disconnect internally—like there's this uncomfortable gap between what, with a slip of the tongue, we call our "Christian" or "church" stuff and what we might call our "normal" or "real" lives.

We have experienced how Jesus has transformed our lives and the lives of others, and we know that he is the answer to the hopelessness we see around us. But like a car stuck in the mud, we're struggling to get traction. As individuals and as churches, we're pressing down the pedal, revving loudly, with wheels spinning furiously, but through all the smoke and smell of burning rubber, rather than advancing forwards, we wonder whether we're just slipping further back. People just seem to be getting on with their lives around us. They're going about their daily business and weekend recreation, and we're struggling to connect, let alone challenge them to stop and think. In Western culture, the Christian faith is a receding memory for many. And for a noisy minority, Christianity is a nightmare that we've now woken up from.

So all things considered, maybe it's more comfortable to retreat to another planet and stay safely out of it. The problem is that this is not where Jesus wants us to be. When he prayed for his disciples, he said to his Father, "My prayer is not that you take them out of the world but that you protect them from the evil one" (John 17 v 15). Yes, Christians are told to live as "foreigners and exiles" in this world (1 Peter 2 v 11). But we're also called to be the "salt of the earth" and "the light of the world" (Matthew 5 v 13-14)—distinctively different to everyone around us but, to those whom God is calling, magnetically attractive.

So what if I was to tell you that the connections are there—indeed, that the connections have always been there? That it *is* possible to bridge the worlds of our friends and our faith? That there are natural connections that can resonate and penetrate deeply, rather than naff ones that simply bounce off the surface?

These connections are not made by some new sales "technique", recent survey or social-science discovery in our quest to be "relevant". Rather they are profoundly theological as we look at our world through God's word. This book is about five themes that, consciously or subconsciously, our culture *and every culture* is talking about. These themes are being lived out in our normal everyday lives, because every human is created by God and therefore exists in relationship to him, be it good or bad. However much it seems to the contrary, our engagement with others is not a "cold-contact" call, because by virtue of them being created, they are in a relationship with God. In other words, God's there and involved long before we are.

These five themes are the "being human" itches that every person has to scratch even though often it makes everything more irritable. And, as we'll see, these are five themes that are both subverted *and* fulfilled in Jesus Christ. There is the closest connection between the world of the gospel and the world of, well, the world. By the power of God's Holy Spirit, we pray that understanding and applying these themes will give us that traction we're looking for to call people to come to Jesus.

Exploring these five themes will also show us that we have more in common with our non-Christian friends and colleagues than we might sometimes feel. That's because these themes are part of being human, which gives us an immediate connection to everyone around us. Yes, Christians are radically different and are called to be radically different. Yes, we are "on another planet", or more biblically, "foreigners and exiles", or "born again", or "in the light" (1 Peter 2 v 11, 23; 1 John 1 v 7). However, we're still human beings—human beings along with those who don't call themselves Christians but who call themselves secular, agnostic, atheist, Muslim, Jedi, nothing at all. Our created human-being-ness is what we have in common possession and means we can always communicate with one another, because our humanity is jointly "ours" and not just "mine" or "yours".

Engaging people with the gospel isn't always easy. It's often hard and painful work. In the amazing, terrifying and Oscar-winning film *Free Solo*, climber Alex Honnold ascends the huge slab of rock El Capitan in Yosemite National Park without any safety aides. There are sections of that climb that are almost vertical and it looks like Alex is walking—Spiderman-style—up glass. But as the camera zooms in, you notice the tiniest little indentation, crack or nub in the surface of the rock, which with incredible imagination and ingenuity Alex turns into a handhold and foothold to make progress. Similarly, in our engagement with our culture we may think it's like walking up glass (and banging our head against a brick wall!), but we know that our common humanity will mean there will always be something to hold onto—something to get a grip on which we can use as a platform for our witness. It's going to take imagination and a great deal of patience, but the point of contact is always there.

In this book, I'm going to show you five of these points of contact—five hidden themes that our culture can't stop talking about, and how they connect to Christ. We'll call them "magnetic points", because they're ideas to which people are irresistibly drawn over and over again. Chapter 2 will outline the biblical framework underpinning this approach. Then, in chapters 3 – 7, we'll look at each of these points in turn, learning how to identify them in the culture around us. In the second half of the book, we'll explore how each of these themes is ultimately and subversively fulfilled in Jesus—and how we can use them to share him with others.

What This Book Is Not (Just) About

I hope I've whetted your appetite in telling you what this book is about. Before we start, I need to say what this book isn't about—or rather, what it isn't just about. This is not just a book about "doing" evangelism or apologetics as if these were separate and specialist Christian activities. It's ironic I say this, because most of the material for this book has been percolating in modules I've taught at Bible college with titles like "Apologetics I" and "Apologetics II" (there's creativity for you!). However, in discussions with my perceptive students, I've increasingly recognised that to siphon off and compartmentalise evangelism and apologetics from Christian discipleship and ministry is artificial and even unhelpful. What Jesus in the Great Commission calls *disciple-making* is nothing other than allowing the gospel to transform every part of our lives.

So our evangelism should flow out of our discipleship, rather than being an add-on activity. If we want to be sharing the gospel in a meaningful, connected way—and if we want to encourage other people in the church to be doing that too—then the starting place is how we frame *our* relationship with Jesus. If my whole life is connected to the gospel, and if I'm growing as a disciple in every part of my life, then the task of connecting the gospel to other people's lives becomes more natural, because we all face common struggles. If I'm applying the gospel to my life so that I have a full, rich relationship with Jesus through all the moments of mundane everyday living, then I'll be able to minister to others. If I'm connecting the dots in *my* everyday story, then I'll be much better equipped to connect the dots in *your* everyday story.

So, this book is not about beating you over the head or guilt-tripping struggling believers to do some huge extra thing. I just want believers to be, well, believers—but in a full, rich way which overflows into and permeates every inch of life, where their love for Jesus just spills out of them. "The mouth speaks what the heart is full of" (Luke 6 v 45). So as we follow Jesus, we invite others to join us on the same path. As it's been said, the Christian is just one beggar telling another beggar where to find bread. When we think like this, we are less likely to come across as morally or intellectually superior or proud but rather as kind and loving. Why? Because our common humanity recognises a solidarity between myself and those with whom I want to share Christ.

The five magnetic points are the longings of our own hearts, not just the hearts of those around us. So as we learn to identify them, understand them and apply the gospel to them, we'll be more excited about Jesus ourselves—and we'll be better equipped to share him with others.

If you want to start speaking of and living for Jesus in a way that draws others to him, this book is for you. This is your invitation to make your faith magnetic.

2. The Cosmic Game of Hide-and-Seek

Have you ever tried asking an old couple who've been married for years about how they first got together? Or, conversely, had the experience of speaking to a couple who have been separated for years about why they broke up?

When it comes to the history of a relationship, who did what, who said what, who started what (and when), often gets lost in the mists of time. We're prone to misremembering things. Sometimes we are happy and thankful to be corrected by that other person. That old couple can giggle, talk over each other and even disagree, while still holding hands. Sometimes, though, we are neither happy nor thankful to be corrected. That couple who separated switch between talking over each other and sitting in stony silence. Particularly in these damaged relationships, there is often a conscious or unconscious forgetfulness on both sides—perhaps they re-interpret events to cover the pain, or maybe even to cause it.

Real relationships (as opposed to mere acquaintances) are messy and mysterious. They can't be summarised in a simple soundbite, and it's very hard to try and disentangle all the spaghetti-like strands of encounters and experiences that make that relationship what it is. And when it comes to remembering the history of any relationship, we all have our take.

The history of the relationship between human beings and the God who created them is similarly messy and complex. That's because we are talking about a personal relationship between the Creator and the creations who bear his image. Humanity and God were both in love once, but now the relationship has fallen apart. Yet if we were to get this "couple" in a room together, God would not be throwing out false accusations, or misrepresenting events, or missing out important details (although *we* sure would be). God has perfect recall and knows in infinite detail who did what, who said what, who started what and when. His "take" is *the* "take". His account is how it *really* was, and how it *really* is, even if we don't like it.

But we don't need to get in a room with God to hear his take. His unflinching but totally fair account is public truth revealed in God's breathed-out word, the Bible. So before we can start making connections between the world of our friends and the world of our faith, we need to get our heads around how they currently stand in relation to each other.

To do that, I want you to cast your mind back for a moment to a game you might have played as a child...

The Cosmic Game of Hide-and-Seek

Imagine that the history of the relationship between God and humanity is like a good old-fashioned game of hide-and-seek. However, in this game the boundaries are not a single room or the whole house ("Just *not* mum and dad's bedroom!") but the entire universe. This is a cosmic game of hide-and-seek.

In the 21st-century West, in *our* version of this history, God is the one who has done the hiding and we are the seekers. And God must have found a great place to hide, because we've looked for him everywhere but he's nowhere to be seen. The Russian astronaut Yuri Gagarin went up into space in 1961 and on his return allegedly told his bosses that he "looked and looked, but I didn't see God".

But even long before that, many of our Western culture shapers had become tired in their increasingly tedious search for God. They'd tried hard to find him, but it just wasn't fun anymore. Shaped by this legacy, many people in our culture today reckon that if God doesn't want to come out, then they don't want to play that game any longer, if they remember the game at all. They think that looking for God is for children, and that as modern people we've progressed and matured beyond it: "We are all grown up now," we tell ourselves.

Whether we conclude that God is hiding himself or just not there at all, it leads us to the same place, practically speaking. With God now firmly out of the picture, it becomes more interesting, more honest and more satisfying to focus on ourselves and the other things around us, and to offer explanations as to why humanity might have dreamt up this game in the first place. Of course, we still search: we search for satisfaction, identity, fulfilment and even legitimacy. But rather than waste time in a futile search for someone who isn't there, we believe we can discover these things by searching closer to home—by looking around us and looking within us.

God's account of cosmic hide-and-seek is a little different:

The wrath of God is being revealed from heaven against all the godlessness and wickedness of people, who suppress the truth by their wickedness, since what may be known about

God is plain to them, because God has made it plain to them.
For since the creation of the world God's invisible qualities—
his eternal power and divine nature—have been clearly seen,
being understood from what has been made, so that people are
without excuse.

For although they knew God, they neither glorified him as God
nor gave thanks to him, but their thinking became futile and
their foolish hearts were darkened. Although they claimed to be
wise, they became fools and exchanged the glory of the immortal
God for images made to look like a mortal human being and
birds and animals and reptiles. (Romans 1 v 18-23)

God is not hiding. Indeed, from the beginning he has been
revealing himself in everything that's been made. His
fingerprints and DNA are all over the scene, including on—
no, *especially* on—his image-bearers, that is, you and me
and every person that's ever lived. Human beings have been
created uniquely to be God's *representatives* and to *rule* under
his overall authority. God is a speaker and maker, and so we
are speakers and makers. We are made to *relate* and we are
made to *cultivate* (that's what my previous book *Plugged In* is
all about).

Look back again at Romans 1. What is it that God has revealed
about himself? We are told in verse 20 that two "invisible"
qualities of God have been impressed upon us: God's "eternal
power" and "divine nature". That's odd. We ought to ask: why
these two things in particular? It's because they highlight two
fundamental aspects of the relationship between the Creator
and the creature, and the distinction between them.

God's "eternal power" points to the recognition that human
creatures are *dependent* upon God's power, as indeed is the
whole of creation. He is all-powerful and all-powering. As

Paul says elsewhere in Acts 17 v 28, "In him we live and move and have our being". To acknowledge our dependence recognises God's upholding and our being held—yet not pinned to the ground so much as cradled in his arms. Dependence recognises God's gracious giving of life and breath and everything; it moves us to receive these gifts with grateful thanks and praise.

By "divine nature", we sense first God's otherness—his divinity. But notice this is a divine *nature*. That is, God is not a "thing" or an "it" but a "someone". This is a personal God and that means a personal relationship, like that of a child to a parent. To quote Paul again in Acts 17 v 28, "We are his offspring". And as in the relationship of the child to a parent, not only is there dependence but there is *accountability*. He is God, and we are not—and as his creatures we owe him an account for how we live in his world. We have the dignity of *being* responsible (we are not robots), but we will also be *held* responsible for the choices we make.

To summarise: God has made it clear in everything that has been made that he is present and we are dependent, and that he is personal and we are accountable. It's so "plain" and "clearly seen" that we don't have any excuses (Romans 1 v 18-19). We can't say we can't see, and we can't say we don't know. In our cosmic game of hide-and-seek, God is not hiding. *We are hiding.*

Do you remember the first game of hide-and-seek?

Then the man and his wife heard the sound of the LORD God as he was walking in the garden in the cool of the day, and they hid from the LORD God among the trees of the garden. But the LORD God called to the man, "Where are you?"

> He answered, "I heard you in the garden, and I was afraid
> because I was naked; so I hid." (Genesis 3 v 8-10)

From their beginning, Adam and Eve knew God. He had created them, he cared for them, provided for them and spoke to them. They were built to be thankful worshippers, dependent upon God and accountable to him. But in listening to and believing in Satan's "take" on the world, which was lies, they made God out to be a liar, rebelled against his authority and grasped at independence. They thought that Satan's "take" offered something better, but in the aftermath of their disobedience they were still as dependent and accountable as they were before, *and they knew this*. The guilt and shame that followed their fall is why they hid. God calling out and asking where they were was not about discovering their location (he's God after all). Rather, it was God *calling them out*. In fact, it was God *calling the whole human race out*. As we learn in the New Testament, not only is the fall of Adam, our representative, counted against us, but we are all born with rebel hearts wanting independence from God and not wanting to be accountable (Romans 5 v 12). It's no game. It's sad, it's bad, and it's mad.

Suppression and Substitution

Our passage in Romans 1 is a commentary on this one event in Genesis 3 and on the repeated cycle of behaviour that it kicked off.

First, we *suppress* the truth in our wickedness (Romans 1 v 18), like someone violently holding a person's head under the water in order to drown them. We don't want to hear that God is powerful and personal, and that we are dependent and accountable, so we get that big fat marker pen and graffiti over God's "take" on the world with our own "take". As in any broken relationship, we conveniently mishear and forget, not because we are honest seekers but because we are expert and ingenious hiders. We hate to think that we are dependent and accountable, so we tell ourselves that we're not; we hate to feel shame and guilt, so we tell ourselves that we don't need to.

Second, as we suppress, we simultaneously *substitute* God and exchange him for all kinds of created things (v 23). This is what the Bible calls idolatry. Idolatry turns good things into "god-things". Being made in God's image means we are instinctive worshippers. So when we try to smother reality, we end up making new twisted "realities" which we are devoted to instead. Often we imagine that these realities are less powerful and less personal, which means that we are less dependent, more in control and less accountable. Again, we are extremely creative in the things we consider, commit to and worship as "ultimate".

And here's where I'm getting to with this: the instinct to suppress the truth and substitute it with other ideas is seen in our culture. The "stories" we humans tell one another— whether that's through boxsets, books, ads, viral videos, or simply the everyday conversations we have with our colleagues—all spin our own account of what's going on in the world, and what matters most.

This all makes for pretty grim reading. We're broken and our relationship with God is broken. But this is where the relational messiness comes in. It's complex, but that's relationships for you.

Let's take our *suppression* of the truth. God speaks to us, and we speak over God. But this isn't a one-off event. It's not static but dynamic. Day after day, God continues to reveal himself through all the details of our lived experiences, and we continue to suppress it. Reveal, suppress, reveal, suppress: it's like a choreographed *Strictly Come Dancing* or *Dancing with the Stars* routine. Moreover, however much we suppress the truth, reality is stubborn and has a habit of getting in the way. Even as rebels we are still God's image-bearers, as dependent upon God and as accountable to him as we ever were. The image of God in us is like one of those inextinguishable birthday candles from the joke shop. No matter how hard we try and blow it out, it always flickers back on.

And what about our *substituting*? Well, our idolatry (and the cultural "stories" which express them) is like a nightmare which has taken ordinary things we've encountered during the day and given them a monstrous and grotesque life of their own as we sleep, spinning a story which takes us further away from reality and further away from God. However, because we are only creatures and not God, there are limits to our creativity. We can't make stories out of nothing. The idols we create and inflate, and the stories we tell about them and ourselves, are mimics of God, his character and his work. They are dress-up divinities and designer deities. They are pretend wannabees who we've pushed onto the stage and into the limelight, a place that should only be reserved for God. Like those desperate parents waiting in the wings of the talent show, we want these idols to be the real thing but in the end they fall flat on their face. They're fakes. They don't have eternal power or divine nature, because they are created and not the Creator. But we try so, so hard to make them fit, because we're made for worship and we just can't escape our createdness: *something has to fill that gap!*

A Messy Mix

Confused? Don't worry—it's not you, it's how it is. It's how we are. Describing it has made the best theologians scratch their heads. Ever since the entrance of sin into the world, human beings have been deeply conflicted creatures. We both *know* God and *don't know* him (v 21); we are running away and hiding from God, and yet there is still a sense, as God's image-bearers, in which we are running *to* him. In our sin and rebellion we don't want the real thing, and yet the way we dress our idols and spin our stories—in our music, books, TV, films, ads, sport, social media and more—shows that we do want the real thing.

As I've said, it's messy and mysterious because we're messy and mysterious, and our relationship with God is messy and mysterious. However, I think we instinctively feel this complexity. Just as we aren't satisfied with one-dimensional portrayals of relationships on the TV because they don't ring true, any simplistic attempt to explain humanity's relationship with God isn't going to satisfy either. There's an authenticity in what I'm describing here. And that shouldn't surprise us, because I'm only describing God's take in Scripture! This is how things really are.

So where does that leave us as Christian disciples? How can we possibly start to get our heads around this ourselves—let alone explain it to our non-Christian friends and neighbours? If only there was a way of making sense of this relational mess that would give us the tools to understand the objects of worship around us, and the traction to proclaim Christ. If only there was a way to unearth the truth that's being suppressed and substituted, and hold it up to a watching world.

Well I think there is...

The Magnetic Points

Let me introduce you to one of my heroes. J.H. Bavinck was a Dutch pastor, missionary to Indonesia and theologian, who lived in the first half of the 20th century. Bavinck's understanding of messy human beings was very much like the one I've been describing. He read the Bible closely and focused on the same passages we've looked at. Bavinck also read his context very closely and studied anthropology and psychology. He knew a lot about other religious traditions and the people committed to them.[1] Putting these two things together, he began to observe some similar patterns in the very different religious traditions he was living among in Indonesia and the Netherlands. It's worth listening to him at this point:

"There seems to be a kind of framework within which human religions need to operate. There appear to be definite points of contact around which all kinds of ideas crystallize. There seem to be quite vague feelings—one might better call them direction signals—that have been actively brooding everywhere … magnetic points that time and again irresistibly compel human religious thought. Human beings cannot escape their power but must provide an answer to those basic questions posed to them. They can answer them with foolish myths, with fairy tales, with totally unique thought-forms, but they cannot ignore them. They impose themselves on people, and in one way or another people must come clean about them." [2]

Bavinck discerns five of these magnetic points—these themes to which we humans are repeatedly drawn. I hope he wouldn't mind, but I've given them my own titles:

- Totality: a way to connect?

- Norm: a way to live?

- Deliverance: a way out?

- Destiny: a way we control?

- Higher power: a way beyond?

These magnetic points act as a kind of "religious anatomy" of fallen human beings who both know God and don't know him *at the same time*. Or to put it another way, these are five permanent "itches" that in our work, rest and play, we have to vigorously scratch.

It's these magnetic points that we are going to focus on for the rest of this book, applying them not so much to those belonging to established "religions", as Bavinck did, but rather to your average "secular" Westerner today. Although we will look at each point separately, they need to be viewed as different perspectives from which to look at people as fallen image-bearers. We'll see that the five points connect to each other in interesting ways. Moreover, they all connect to God's revelation of his eternal power (and our dependency) and divine nature (and our accountability) that we saw in Romans 1 v 20. Crucially, the magnetic points also wonderfully connect to God's *full* revelation of himself in the person and work of Jesus Christ (that's running ahead of ourselves, though).

Over the next five chapters, I will briefly describe each magnetic point in question, then show what it looks like in cultural examples (because I do think there is truth in the motto drummed into writers and filmmakers, "show don't tell"). Some of these examples are my own, but many have been given to me by students and those in churches and conferences with whom I have test-driven this material and for whom I'm profoundly grateful. The point is that I want you quickly to get used to spotting these magnetic points in your own context. The cultural examples I give here will be very quickly out of date, but the tools will, I hope and pray, last you a lifetime.

Up front, I want to say that looking at the world through the prism of these magnetic points might seem a little awkward at first. It's a bit like getting a new pair of glasses. If, like me, you wear glasses all the time, you'll know what a big deal it can be when it's time for a new pair. My wife Elly doesn't wear glasses, which means she just doesn't get it. When I come back from the opticians with a new pair of glasses, Elly invariably doesn't notice. When I, mildly traumatised, point out the dramatic change to my appearance, she just shrugs and says that they look like every other pair!

The thing about getting a new pair of glasses is that for the first few hours you see something new in your field of vision that is awkward and distracting: the frames. After a while you don't see the glasses themselves but rather you see *through* the glasses. So it is with these magnetic points. It might be hard work at the beginning, but after a while it will become more natural and you'll see examples of these points everywhere—like "earworms", but "eyeworms" (although, thinking about it, that does sound pretty disgusting).

So, as I describe these magnetic points and give examples, try to think of your own examples from your life and your surroundings: the things you watch, read and listen to, and the people you speak to day to day. How do these examples show our hiding and our seeking? How do they scratch the itch, but not satisfactorily—indeed, how do they make things more irritated? Finally, start thinking about how these examples might relate to Jesus and his way of viewing the world.

Bad Hider, Best Seeker

Have you ever played hide-and-seek with a three-year-old? They tend to be pretty bad at it. They hide, but as you enter the room, they just can't resist giving away their position with a stifled giggle or even a full "here I am" jump out. Even when you patiently explain the game again ("It's *hide* and seek"), they still do it, over and over again.

I don't want to be disrespectful but when it comes to our cosmic game of hide-and-seek, just like a three-year-old, God is not good at hiding:

In the past God spoke to our ancestors through the prophets at many times and in various ways, but in these last days he has spoken to us by his Son, whom he appointed heir of all things, and through whom also he made the universe. The Son is the radiance of God's glory and the exact representation of his being, sustaining all things by his powerful word. (Hebrews 1 v 1-3)

No one has ever seen God, but the one and only Son, who is himself God and is in the closest relationship with the Father, has made him known. (John 1 v 18)

In Jesus Christ, God is jumping up and down, waving his hands and saying, "Here I am, look, it's me". And what do we do? We don't recognise him. We ignore him. We reject him.

No, God's not hiding... *but he's the best seeker.*

When I was a kid I played hide-and-seek with my mum and dad. I found a great place to hide, right at the back of the sofa. What I couldn't understand was why the sound of my parents' laughter after five minutes became sounds of terror after 50. By that point I was so worried I'd be in trouble that I wasn't going to come out for anyone. And then, after what seemed like ages, my dad bent right down with his eye to the ground and peered under that sofa. He must have seen the edge of my sock, because he reached his arm out and he pulled:

For the Son of Man came to seek and to save the lost.
(Luke 19 v 10)

PART 1

The Magnetic Points

3. TOTALITY
A Way to Connect?

In north London, about a quarter of a mile from Oak Hill College, the seminary where I live and work, is a theatre called Chickenshed. It's well-known locally for its inclusive work with children and young people from diverse backgrounds. During the early days of the COVID-19 pandemic in 2020, when the lockdown meant we were allowed out for exercise only once a day, I headed out for a walk around mid-morning. On my way I passed the Chickenshed's large advertising hoarding which usually displays its upcoming shows. Of course, because of COVID-19 the theatre had been recently closed, and there was no traffic and no other pedestrians to be seen, making the whole scene feel eerily like some post-apocalyptic dystopian film. A banner had been draped over the hoarding, declaring in big bold lettering:

UBUNTU
translated simply as "humanity"
or "the belief in a universal bond of sharing that
connects all humanity".
Chickenshed will continue to strive to connect all people
and all communities.
I am because we are.

I continued to walk another half a mile and came to Cockfosters tube station. The bus stop opposite the station, which would normally have a queue of people in front of it, displayed the following poster that had been put up around the time of the Brexit debate. Referring to the fact that good escalator etiquette on London's underground demands that you stand to the right, it said:

> Born here or not,
> if you know to stand on the right,
> you're a Londoner.
> We are not an island.
> We're home to so much more.
>
> HSBC UK | Together we thrive

I was expecting a quiet walk, but what I got were effectively two preaches within two minutes of each other. They both expressed our first magnetic point: totality.

Part of the Whole

The idea of totality is centred around connection. It asks questions like: Who are we as human beings? What's our place in the universe? Are we worth more than just the elements of our body, which if added up and sold wouldn't even give me enough change to buy two flat whites? Are we worthless specks, or are we inherently valuable? Is there, as that theatre banner put it, a universal bond which connects us all?

As humans, we have an innate sense of totality: that we are connected and part of something much bigger. We are part of a whole (a "totality"). We are small cogs in a much bigger machine; tiny cells that are part of a bigger organism, and cosmically interconnected. We have this sense that we do not stand alone as islands in the universe but somehow belong to something bigger, something greater. It's the recognition that we want to feel *a part* of the universe and have some solidarity and connection with it. At the same time, we also need to know we are *apart* from the universe, lest we lose our individuality, our identity, our "me-ness", and end up being swallowed up by the whole.

This means that with this sense of totality comes a tension. On the one hand, we may feel completely and totally insignificant, powerless and without value. Some of you may have experienced this, especially if you are more existentially angsty. I remember being in the sea once while on holiday. Just looking at the vast expanse of the ocean in front of me gave me a weird tummy-wobble: "Who am *I*, this miniscule speck?"

But contemplating totality can also be a positive experience too. It's that feeling you get when you have an experience of connection—that sense that together, we are powerful and significant. We are a part of something bigger. We do have meaning. We do have a place. We are matter that matters! Indeed, at the high point of these experiences we feel so "at one" with everything that we feel like masters of the universe—almost divine—because we are the totality. Coming down from the high of an experience like this and getting back on the treadmill of the Monday morning commute can be miserable. We feel lost and abandoned and we desperately crave a taste of totality again and again.

Bavinck says that this idea "has entranced people through all the centuries of human history". And here's why:

"Ordinary human life is always broken, incomplete, insignificant, bungling and banal. As soon as a person approaches that secret border where they leave behind their own individuality

and allows themselves to be engulfed by all that there is, they become great. That is where they experience divine reality, not as something that exists outside themselves but as something that throbs deep within." [3]

Examples of Totality

Most established religious traditions or so-called world religions include an element of opening oneself up to totality, especially if they have a mystical streak. It might be the idea of *satori* (enlightenment) in Japanese Zen Buddhism, or, in certain Indian traditions (that we in the West have labelled as Hinduism), the need to lose one's individuality and ego in Brahman. Interestingly, it's totality that explains why your Hindu friend will not understand why you would want them to convert to Christianity. As the prominent British Hindu Satish Sharma has said:

"When the rain stopped falling, the Ocean gazed out at the puddles on the shore and the puddles gazed at each other and at the Ocean … All 'faiths' which are busy converting are stuck in Puddle vision, trying to separate the Ocean into Puddles and then gathering Puddles to make a big Puddle. They are thus revealed as being unaware of the shared essence, i.e. water. If you are aware of the essence you see the futility of the conversion game." [4]

In Islam, one could talk about the *ummah*, the worldwide community of Muslims, to demonstrate totality. Moreover, there are more mystical strands of Islamic tradition. Bavinck was familiar with some of these from his time in Indonesia: "People speak there of the 'ocean of Allah,' of 'the mixing of Lord and servant' which takes place in mystical ecstasy."[5]

I find this all fascinating, but it's not the focus of this book! Of course, there are thousands of Muslims, Hindus, Buddhists and Sikhs in the UK and US and the magnetic points remain relevant in our understanding and witness to these neighbours. However, I'm thinking more of the majority in the West and their relationship with totality—the kind of people that wouldn't call themselves "religious" but maybe "secular", "atheist", "agnostic", or perhaps "spiritual". These are women, men and children who have breathed the air of a culture whose theme song has been John Lennon's *Imagine*, where "above us [is] only sky". People who, in the words of another preacher, the author of Ecclesiastes, believe there is only life "under the sun" and nothing else. As I hope to demonstrate, the magnetic point of totality still has to come out somewhere, and it does. We just need to have the right glasses on to see it.

Take, for example, the way that Facebook celebrated its one billionth user with an ad campaign called "The things that connect us". Here is a script to the advert:

"Chairs. Chairs are made so that people can sit down and take a break. Anyone can sit on a chair and, if the chair is large enough, they can sit down together. And tell jokes. Or make up stories. Or just listen.

"Chairs are for people. And that is why chairs are like Facebook.

"Doorbells. Airplanes. Bridges. These are things people use to get together, so they can open up and connect about ideas and music and other things that people share.

"Dance floors. Basketball. A great nation. A great nation is something people build so they can have a place where they belong.

"The Universe. It is vast and dark. And it makes us wonder if we are alone. So maybe the reason we make all of these things is to remind us that we are not."

Obviously Mark Zuckerberg had been reading his J.H. Bavinck. But the ad is getting at something: online groups and identities are one way in which people look for a sense of totality. On the one hand, it helps us feel connected with others in a way which feels safe and inclusive, because everything is one step removed from us and we're in control. However, at the same time, we can also feel powerless and distanced because it's virtual: we're wholly detached from the created or natural order. And often, the online world feels anything but safe and inclusive, with those who say the wrong thing being trolled and publicly shamed. It's a total-ity mess!

At the other end of the spectrum, there is the increasing popularity of tech fasts and digital minimalism, driven by the desire to escape virtual reality and be closer to nature, more "one" with the cosmos. Late in 2018, Jack Dorsey, the co-founder of Twitter exchanged Silicon Valley for a bare-bones retreat at a monastery in Myanmar.[6]

Or consider the recent trend in tracing our family history and the popularity of TV programmes like *Who Do You Think You Are?*, in which celebrities are helped to trace their ancestry. We want to know that we are part of something bigger, to know we have roots, to know that we belong.

What about conspiracy-theory enthusiasts? Such people often believe they are part of a much bigger narrative that others can't see. In a strange way it provides greater significance if you think you are awake to "the matrix" somehow.

Or think about Comic-Con, or Pride marches, or anything where those who often feel like "outsiders" are able to join together. For those participating, there is a real feeling of invulnerability around these sorts of events, because while you *know* you are still one little person—insignificant and vulnerable—you're also surrounded by people who are "on your side". You know you are just one person, but you also sense that all these strangers around you, who you will probably never speak to, would have your back.

More generally, consider the appeal of stadium sporting events or music concerts. Why did we pine for them when they were suspended during the pandemic? Because we know there is something we share together in mass movement like this. Yes, we can sing in our bedroom, yes, we can sing on Zoom, but singing in a stadium with tens of thousands of others is a completely different and elevated experience.

What about our sense of connection to our people and our nation? This is another way in which many of us feel part of a whole—part of a totality. When the 850-year-old Notre-Dame Cathedral was severely damaged by fire in April 2019, there were newspaper headlines like: "Notre-Dame is us, it is Paris, it is the world too". One billion Euros was quickly raised for restoration work. President Macron's speech in the aftermath of the fire described Notre-Dame as "our history" and "the epicentre of our lives", saying, "I am solemnly telling you tonight: this cathedral will be rebuilt by all of us together". What was fascinating was the degree of sentimentality expressed for a religious building from a country that is so avowedly secularist and post-Christian. The Parisians love their cathedral but seemingly want nothing to do with God.

What about the avalanche of adverts on TV and public transport for dating apps: eharmony, Match.com, Silver Singles, HER? In the "above us, only sky" world, romantic relationships often bear the weight that communion with God, as the transcendent being, used to bear. People therefore consider themselves to have a deeper need for a perfect romantic relationship. We're desperate to find and connect with "the one" (in the *Jerry Maguire* "you complete me" sense. If you've not seen the movie, find the scene on YouTube!). At a deep, subconscious level, people know they have been created for close communion with another—and they seek to find it in romantic human relationships.

Let's finish our examples of totality with something a little more literary. Donna Tartt's celebrated novel *The Secret History* is about a secretive group of liberal arts students looking for an experience of hedonistic transcendence. One of the most memorable passages in the book comes from the lips of Julian, their Classics Professor, as he talks about the ancient Greek philosophers' ideas about how to break free of ourselves and connect with true beauty:

"Beauty is terror. Whatever we call beautiful, we quiver before it. And what could be more terrifying and beautiful, to souls like the Greeks or our own, than to lose control completely? To throw off the chains of being for an instant, to shatter the accident of our mortal selves? Euripides speaks of the Maenads: head thrown back, throat to the stars, 'more like deer than human being.' To be absolutely free! One is quite capable, of course, of working out these destructive passions in more vulgar and less efficient ways. But how glorious to release them in a single burst! To sing, to scream, to dance barefoot in the woods in the dead of night, with no more awareness of mortality than an animal! These are powerful mysteries. The bellowing of bulls. Springs of honey bubbling from the ground. If we are strong enough in our souls we can rip away the veil and look that naked, terrible beauty right in the face; let God consume us, devour us, unstring our bones. Then spit us out reborn."[7]

This then is our first magnetic point: totality. Is there a way to connect? What is my relationship with the rest of reality and what does that relationship mean for my identity, individuality and my significance? How is it that I'm both part and apart, a speck and special, nothing and noble? These are the questions to which we keep returning.

4. NORM
A Way to Live?

What's your relationship with rules? Are you instinctively a rule-keeper or a rule-breaker? Perhaps it depends on who makes the rules. And what's your reaction when you break the rules or fall short of what's acceptable? Moreover, what's your attitude when someone else does? Can there be forgiveness, or at least forgetfulness? Or is that "it" for them? Does their stain remain?

If you didn't already know your answers to these questions, surely the year 2020 revealed them more clearly than ever. In the UK at least, the pandemic brought with it a weird and wonderful variety of legal restrictions (which nonetheless required interpretation), strong recommendations (which also required interpretation) and nebulous pleas for "respect" for others (yes, also open to interpretation).

On one particular morning I listened to an unrepentant member of the public calling in to a radio show. He had taken the "executive decision" to meet with eight of his friends for a special anniversary, when legally only six were allowed to meet. When questioned by the show's host, he said that he was a law-abiding citizen, unless the rules happened to be "unjust" or "inconsistent". He was especially disgruntled because he knew there was a zealous neighbour on his street who had reported him to the police—the same neighbour who months earlier had reported another lady on the road for walking her energetic sheepdog three times a day during lockdown, when exercise was only permitted once!

But that wasn't all. We also had #Blacklivesmatter and an earnest public conversation about how we should (or is it must?) respond to racism. What's more, we had to deal with the questions raised when these two things occupied the same space at the same time (namely, is it right to break lockdown in order to attend an anti-racism protest?). With a year like that still in recent memory, I've got a good head start in describing our next magnetic point.

This second magnetic point is called norm and asks whether there is *a way to live*—and how we know what that is. As human beings, we know there are rules to be obeyed. We accept that there are "norms"—moral standards and codes— which come from outside of us but to which we must adhere. Even after we've tried to explain them, and even explain them away (in terms of biology, evolution or anthropology, say), there remains a vague and nagging sense deep down that there are norms of behaviour which apply to all people. One could say they are "transcendent" in that they originate from somewhere beyond life as we know it. The idea that things are ordered on a cosmic scale brings with it a sense of responsibility and also freedom: will we choose to live up to those norms or not?

Bavinck describes our relationship with the norm like this:

"I can never do what I please with awareness of the norm, but that awareness of the norm can do whatever it pleases with me.

It can bring me to despair, it can cast me down. It can hound into me unmentionable despair and fear. If I ignore awareness of the normative, awareness of the normative never ignores me; it refuses to let me avoid it. It is not the case that I am the king and the norm is my servant, but the norm is king and I am the accused and the guilty party. The awareness of the normative always contains something from the realm of the divine. This is why all sorts of attempts to explain it as arising from human conventions, from slowly developing customs, from cutting a deal, and from nurture, all hopelessly fail." [8]

Examples of Norm

Bavinck wrote that over 70 years ago. Maybe you're thinking: *Surely we've moved on as a society since then? Aren't we less concerned with "norms" now?*

I'm not so sure. I'd say that we are as "norming" as we ever were, it's just that the norms have changed. A friend of mine was in their local coffee shop the other day and a lady walked in pushing a buggy. As she walked up to the counter she asked, "Are your straws paper or plastic?" Fortunately the owner said paper, at which the lady said, "I'm so glad I can drink here". For many of us, being low plastic and environmentally friendly is the new norm—or standard—that we aspire to live up to.

What's more, social media (not around in Bavinck's time) whips up and magnifies the norm. Today it's not enough to be virtuous; we need to be *seen* to be virtuous (hence the phenomenon of "virtue signalling"). Therefore, I would argue that our Western post-Christian culture seems to be wrestling with this magnetic point more than ever, even though it doesn't realise it. You could easily play a game of "norm bingo" with your friends where you spot as many instances as you can.

The norm is very much alive and kicking—in fact, it's tying us up in knots. We are drawn to the norm but, to use a cooking analogy, the consistency of our norm, like my gravy, is a little grainy.

For instance, people are struggling to reconcile their professed commitment to freedom, inclusion and tolerance with their insistence that the beliefs of certain individuals or groups are evil and have no place being expressed in today's society. I'm not the first person to comment that tolerance used to mean the idea of "bearing with" or "putting up with" someone with whom you disagreed. Now tolerance has become, frankly, an *intolerance* towards anyone who disagrees with me. "Bearing with" has become "bearing down", and "putting up" has become "shutting up".

Or consider this: one of the characteristics of Gen Z's passion for social justice is that it evidences a strong anti-authoritarian trend, but at the same time it voices a strong demand for people in authority to enforce their norms! And then what are we to make of the popularity of psychologist Jordan Peterson and his book *12 Rules for Life* telling us to take responsibility? It screams of a generation who want to know how to live! It's all so confused and so confusing and demonstrates that we know, on the one hand, that there is a transcendent universal norm and that we want people to adhere to it, and on the other hand, that we do not want to adhere to it ourselves. We can't live with the norm and we can't live without the norm.

There are major societal implications with all this. The ambition to make public discourse a "safe space" for everyone may well demonstrate a desire to protect the vulnerable, but banning all speech that challenges consensus creates its own dangers. Columnist Rory Sutherland exposes the contradiction by comparing "safe spaces" to quiet carriages in trains:

"The quiet carriage, when you think of it, is akin to the idea of a safe space. Just as in a quiet carriage the rules are set by the single most neurotic person on the train, in a "safe space", the terms of acceptable discourse are set by the thinnest-skinned 0.01 per cent of the population. And like the quiet carriage, this simply does not work. Just as you can't run a restaurant which serves only food to which nobody is allergic, a space which annoys no one becomes intolerable to everyone." [9]

But lest you think that I'm unfairly taking aim at a certain stereotype of Gen-Z social justice warriors, let me be clear: people who work in suits wrestle with the norm too. Take, for example, work appraisal systems. One person told me about how his company, like many secular employers, officially praise and promote innovation and risk-taking, and say that they want their employees to be free to be themselves, to express themselves, and to work in ways that suit them. Each week, this guy and his colleagues are told that this is what they are to aspire to. However, every year, the appraisal system insists on evaluating each person on a static grid of numerical scores that makes no room for nuances in job descriptions or personality. It turns out that everyone must work in exactly the same way in order to get a good score. And when your appraisal score determines your pay for the next twelve months, the practical upshot is that employees spend the whole year in a state of tension between following the rules of individualism and the rules of the appraisal statistics.

What about clothing? A friend of mine was a goth in her youth. Part of the appeal was being different to the norm, but the other side of it was that she and her friends were all different together, in the same way. The goth rules were very different to the rules of the wider culture, but they were there (for example, she remembers that really well-established goths could wear baby pink, because it was "ironic", but if you wore it without the right credentials, you'd show yourself up as not fitting in). The appeal of being a goth lies in not conforming to certain societal norms, but you still want to conform to the rules of the subculture, because you need to fit in somewhere.

A few years ago there was even a (slightly ironic) fashion trend called normcore—defined as a bland "anti-style" where you'd dress in a conventional, nondescript way.[10] (Jerry Seinfeld and Steve Jobs seem to have been fashion role models as far as I can tell!). According to one fashion editor: "Normcore moves away from a coolness that relies on difference to a post-authenticity coolness that opts in to sameness. But instead of appropriating an aestheticized version of the mainstream, it just cops to the situation at hand. To be truly Normcore, you need to understand that there's no such thing as normal."[11] Confused? Me too!

And now for something completely different. I'm a big West Ham United Football Club fan. At the beginning of the 2019-2020 season, there was a lot of controversy surrounding the introduction of video assistant referee (VAR) technology to the British Premier League. Around that time, I was at a home game against Brighton where there was an incident referred to VAR which seemed to go on for ever. What I didn't realise until later was that another West Ham fan Daisy Christodoulou was in the stadium tweeting a long thread during this stop in play. Not only does this thread dispel any caricatures you might have about West Ham United fans, it speaks directly to our topic of the norm in showing the complexities of how a society decides where to draw lines and, moreover, the complexities in working out how fine that line should be.

"I'm at the Olympic Stadium and there is a break for a VAR check. It's going on for a while, so I thought I'd take the opportunity to jot down a few thoughts about VAR.

"What I find fascinating about VAR is how it perfectly encapsulates many wider 21st century preoccupations: the promises & limitations of rationality, the tensions between the rule of law, experts, crowds & tradition, and the challenges of finding meaning in late modernity.

"The promise of VAR is simple: more right decisions. In practice, it complicates the very notion of "right". What is a handball? What is offside? What is "clear and obvious"? Ultimately, what is truth?

"The most traditional view of refereeing is that the referee's decision IS the right decision. That is, there is no such thing as an offside goal. If the referee gave it as offside, it WAS offside. His decision is final.

"VAR completely destabilises this, and instead introduces the idea of a correct objective reality which technology will bring us closer to than one human on-field referee. But of course, the evidence from that technology still has to be interpreted by humans.

"So in the worst-case scenario, VAR undermines the legitimacy of human judgement without replacing it with anything better. Far from removing arbitrary human judgement, VAR simply emphasises just how arbitrary it is.

"This aspect of VAR reminds me of nothing so much as German Higher Biblical criticism [an 18th and 19th branch of Biblical

studies intent on getting behind the text of Scripture]. If we apply the latest scientific & technological tools to the excavation of Biblical meaning, we'll get closer to what God meant. Or we might just blow up the foundations on which it all rests....

"...As @HelenHet20 says, crowds want big truths, not small ones. VAR succeeds not if it gets 'more right decisions', but if fans & players think it improves the game. Like most governance, it's about consensus. If people think VAR is working, it's working. If they don't, it's not.

"Cricket (& rugby & tennis) show tech can work. Why is it not working so well in football? Is it teething problems? Is it football's arrogance, not learning the lessons from other sports? Yes, partly. But another problem is, paradoxically, the simplicity of football's rules.

"Rugby and cricket have far more complex rules than football, yet have adopted technology with much greater success. You might have expected the opposite. But perhaps it is football's very simplicity which works against it.

"What VAR reveals is that for decades we have all been relying on a great deal of tacit knowledge in the interpretation of football's rules. 'Clear and obvious' is not clear and obvious. Even handball, the rule that practically defines the game, is not obvious.

"In any field you can think of, technology is bad at solving problems which require tacit knowledge: that is, knowledge of all those things that exist, but that cannot be codified.

"The risk is that football's intrinsic simplicity is unsustainable in an era of technological complexity. Attempts to get more right decisions will unravel the consensus on which the game is based & reveal the essential absurdity of our obsession with it.

"The comparisons with 19th century Christianity are stark. Is football dead?" [12]

Wow! And there was I, inanely booing over the time it was taking to make the decision. (The match ended in a frustrating 3-3 draw, if you're interested.) But notice what Christodoulou is saying about how we approach the norm, particularly if we think technology and "the science" will always make this clearer and simpler. Headline news: they won't.

We could go on. Take the trend in "open marriages" and other alternative forms of non-monogamy. Yet even as this tries to pull away from marriage's roots—of one man and one woman—it still has "norms" of its own, for example, the need for an agreement to "allow for" promiscuity.

Once again, let's finish with a book. *Broken Homes* by Ben Aaronovitch is the fourth book in his *Rivers of London* series, an urban fantasy about a police officer who gets recruited to a lesser-known, magically-focused branch of the Metropolitan Police. In this quotation, we see once again our need for the norm in all levels of society.

"Policing, whatever else you've heard, is by consent.

"Even hardened professional villains consent to be policed. This is clear from the way they complain that nonces, rapists and bankers get shorter sentences than decent ordinary criminals. It's the same with all the other criminals, the weekend shoplifters, the drunk drivers, the overexcited protestors and executives who pop into the loo for a quick snort. When it's their stuff that goes walkies, or their car that's damaged, when their kids go missing and their briefcases get snatched, they all seem to be pretty consensual about the police. Everyone consents to the police. It's just the operational priorities they argue about." [13]

In one sense, this whole chapter has been a discussion over "operational priorities" on a society-wide level. And that's the magnetic point known as norm.

5. DELIVERANCE
A Way Out?

"We welcome you to an Olympic Opening Ceremony for everyone. A ceremony that celebrates the creativity, eccentricity, daring and openness of the British genius by harnessing the genius, creativity, eccentricity, daring and openness of modern London. We hope ... that through all the noise and excitement you'll glimpse a single golden thread of purpose—the idea of Jerusalem—of the better world, the world of real freedom and true equality, a world that can be built through the prosperity of industry, through the caring nation that built the welfare state, through the joyous energy of popular culture, through the dream of universal communication. A belief that we can build Jerusalem. And that it will be for everyone." (Director Danny Boyle, writing in the 2012 Summer Olympics Opening Ceremony Programme)

That was the dream almost a decade ago when London hosted the 2012 Olympics. It was a summer when, in the words of one politician, "Britain was crop-dusted with serotonin".[14]

I'll let you come to your own conclusions as to what extent that dream has been realised.

Our third magnetic point is arguably the most obvious. We will call it deliverance. It asks whether there is *a way out*. We know there is something not right with the world. The problems of brokenness, wrongdoing, suffering and death consistently confront us. Sometimes we look forward to a future where things will be better. At other times we look back; we mourn for a "paradise lost" and yearn for deliverance from these evils, craving release and redemption. In this sense, the way out is a way back. We know that in this world, troubles do not melt like lemon drops. Yet when Ariana Grande gave a soaring stadium rendition of *Somewhere Over the Rainbow* in a benefit concert for the victims of a terrorist bombing, it spoke to our inbuilt and God-given recognition that our home as we currently know it is simply not enough. There is more—there must be more. Something is broken and it needs fixing. Such songs are just another example of what has long been labelled in literature and psychology as *Sehnsucht*: a sense of mystical longing and yearning for happiness and fulfilment in the face of a reality which does not provide it.

Examples of Deliverance

With this magnetic point of deliverance comes a number of questions we gnaw at: What do we need to be delivered from? What is this new, redeemed state we long for? Can *I* bring it about myself? Can we bring it about together? Or will we only find deliverance in coming to terms with the fact that we can't be delivered?

Of course, the answers to these questions are diverse—and often depend on what it is we think we need delivering from.

If our ultimate problem is ignorance, then deliverance comes through education. In *The Secret Reason We Eat Meat*, psychologist Dr Melanie Joy argues that we can only be delivered from the deceptive and violent ideology of "carnism" (as opposed to vegetarianism and veganism), by awareness:

"Awareness is the light that shines through the fog of carnism, illuminating the dark truths the system tries hard to hide from us. Awareness cuts through the cloudy haze in our minds, dispelling the shadow that's been cast on our hearts, and realising the natural glow of our empathy. Awareness is the greatest threat to carnism because with awareness we can make choices that reflect what we authentically think and feel, rather than what we have been told to think and feel. We can make our choices freely. Without awareness, there is not free choice." [15]

If the problem is a virus, let's call it coronavirus, then "the science" must be the answer. In his first speech as US President-elect, Joe Biden pledged "to marshal the forces of hope and the forces of science in the great battles of our time".[16] Meanwhile the UK Prime Minister Boris Johnson declared in characteristic style that "We are shining the light of science on this virus, and we will defeat this devilish disease."[17] (Is it me or does there seem to be a lot of light being shone around?)

If loss of identity is the problem, then nationalism will bring deliverance. If loneliness is the problem, then community will bring deliverance. If discrimination is the problem, then justice is the answer—or is that education again? Indeed, can equality only be delivered through structural change from the top, or is the onus on us all to deliver salvation?

It is difficult not to notice in our society the increasing critique of free speech in universities, the death of the traditional political debate in the public square, and its replacement by the denouncement and demonisation of the "other". Isn't this about deliverance though—an attempt to cleanse the world of evil by exclusively human judgment and exclusion, hoping that use of the law will bring about the necessary change in society?

Perhaps the problem is not "out there" but "in here", within me. The book *The Chimp Paradox* presents a "mind management model" created by Steve Peters, a psychiatrist who has transformed the careers of many of our sporting heroes. In this model, we come to understand that the problem is ourselves and the solution to the problem is ourselves. We long to be in a place where we are not controlled by our desires—our inner "Chimp"—and must save ourselves from our own brain. Interestingly, in Peters' view the impulsive part of your brain, your "Chimp", is not "you".

This is all quite heavy stuff. Of course, one way to deal with thinking about deliverance is not to. Drinking and drug use is an obvious way to anaesthetise ourselves and thereby "escape". One can also be "delivered" from reality by distraction and diversion. A pastor friend of mine told me that he's currently discipling two guys in their 30s who are addicted to the game "Clash of Clans" on their mobile phones, simply because it is a way to escape their lives. Running away, though, is not as easy as it sounds. Even in our "escape" we are still haunted by these same questions, or better, drawn to them. Having finally been made by my kids to sit and watch Marvel's *Avengers* films, I don't have to be the most incisive film critic to note that desire for deliverance looms large as a recurrent theme.

If Marvel films aren't your thing then how about deliverance in classical music? In a revealing conversation a few years ago, the journalist Tom Service interviewed the pianist Murray Perahia, who is considered one of the world's greatest living pianists.[18] At one point Perahia talks about the great composers being able, often at a subconscious level, to touch us in a way that enables a melting of mind and heart. For Perahia, his performances need to have some kind of story and narrative. There has to be what musicians call tonality: a sense motion, with the music going somewhere, a process of arrival and leaving, coming and going, consonance and dissonance, but with a keynote—or "tonic note"—which it keeps coming "home" to. In this way, classical music taps into our looking back/looking forward sense of *Sehnsucht*. In Perahia's opinion, the reason that much contemporary classical music has lost its way is because it lacks tonality— and tonality is what we humans are wired for. It's "native to us as human beings, we need tonality because it's our compass, it's the only way, I think, we hear music ... I think people need tonality, that's why the [great] composers used it because they knew we needed it."

Our Greatest Fear

Yet behind all our culture's longings for deliverance there often lurks a darker fear. In the critically acclaimed black comedy *I Hate Suzie*, Billie Piper plays Suzie Pickles, an actress and celebrity whose life and relationships are thrown into utter disarray as compromising pictures of her appear in the media. The final episode of the series begins with Suzie in a recording studio sound booth doing a voiceover for a phone company called EBG: "Here at EBG we don't just take care of your phone, we now provide for your electricity, heating and gas. EBG. Everything is home." Suzie keeps on having to do multiple takes because there is not enough "warmth" coming through. As the sound engineer points out, "There's a sadness in your voice". He pauses for a moment and then continues:

*"Imagine you're a god. It's always the same: the text is, 'Buy this'.
The subtext is, 'You're never going to die'. Ok? Do one like that
and we can go home."*

There is a lot of truth in that. And although we constantly
seek assurances to the contrary, the stubborn fact of death
casts a long shadow over the magnetic point of deliverance.

Sometimes this fear is obvious. I know lots of pastors who
have had many conversations with both Christians and non-
Christians for whom sickness and death is their main anxiety
point. One person was anxious because his dad and sister
had cancer, so he may well get it as well. Another because she
had had a heart attack and also lost a baby in a miscarriage.
Another because she grew up in a family where her sister was
in and out of hospital a lot. For these people, dark thoughts
are always with them, convincing them that they're going to
die soon. Every cough or lump or pain is dreadful. We probably
know more people like this than we realise because they're
unlikely to tell us that's how they feel, out of a sense of shame.

And as our society drifts further from its Christian heritage,
there is an increasing sense of utter confusion and lostness
in this area. A friend had a long conversation with another
dog walker recently who was struggling to come to terms with
the death of a loved one and had dabbled with spiritualist
things. When my friend spoke of the hope of resurrection,
this well-read urbanite responded: "But how can we know? If
only someone could come back from the other side to tell us
for certain..." Similarly, someone recently sent me a picture
of a padlock he'd found, tied to a barbed-wire fence along a
coastal path where lots of people go to appreciate the wonder
of creation. The inscription on the padlock read: "If love could
have saved you, you would have lived forever. You were too

beautiful for earth. Love mummy and daddy." We sense that death is both desperately sad yet frighteningly inevitable.

While much of our popular culture operates like the EBG ad in *I hate Suzie*, subtly telling us that everything will be ok really, some creatives choose instead to confront death head on. *Totentanz* ("Dance of Death") is Thomas Adès' critically acclaimed composition for mezzo-soprano, baritone and orchestra, which premiered at the BBC proms in 2013. At once arresting and macabre, the work sets to music an anonymous German text that appears under a huge 15th-century frieze which once covered the inside of St Mary's Church, Lübeck. The frieze depicts a danced drama with the character of Death seizing people from every category of society in descending order of status, from pope to peasant to baby. Class and privilege count for nothing.

"Good folk, come, rich or poor, this way,
Come, young and old, to see the play.
And think on this: though every man
Would live forever, no one can." ("The Preacher", Totentanz)

"Oh death, how can I understand?
I cannot walk, yet I must dance!" ("The Baby", Totentanz)

Interviewed about the piece, Adès notes that the dance of death is not optional—it's one we all have to dance. His work is both terrifying and also funny and absurd because of the total powerlessness of everyone, no matter who they are: Death has to tell the pope to take off his hat because it won't fit into the coffin. At the end of the interview Adès is asked whether the writing of the piece has changed his view of mortality. He responds with a chuckle: "No, I mean it wouldn't matter if it had. I mean it's not going to change anything is it? That's the point of the piece."

There are others who might think this attitude is a little defeatist. Perhaps there is a way to be delivered from death. Perhaps we *can* live for ever. Tech magnate Elon Musk is a well-known champion of cryonics, a process which aims to preserve the body until a time in the future when that person could be brought back to life.[19] Speaking to Hack Club (a network of high school coding clubs), here's part of Musk's answer to the question, "Is cryonics legit?"

"I think, assuming that the brain is frozen quickly after death, then I think you probably could extract quite a lot of information from it in the future. And you might be able to create something approximating that person. I mean there's gonna be a few issues obviously. But the brain is very physical. It's much less mysterious than people think. Well, I suppose simultaneously amazing and less mysterious. Neurons are like circuits. They're like physical circuits. So if you have a physical brain, you should be able to recreate those physical circuits. Yeah with some issues of course, because there's going to be some damage."[20]

In other instances, when our culture *does* admit death's existence, we continue to distract ourselves from its harsh reality, reinforcing our bravado in the face of it, whitewashing over the fear that might haunt us if we only stopped to think about it. In an article entitled "How Death Got Cool", Marisa Meltzer shows how "dying well" and "death positivity" is becoming a defining obsession of our time in some sub-cultures.[21]

One of Meltzer's interviewees is mortician Caitlin Doughty, founder of The Order of the Good Death, "a group of funeral industry professionals, academics, and artists exploring ways to prepare a death phobic culture for their inevitable mortality". Members of the order (most of whom appear to be in their twenties and thirties) include a "grave garment designer", a "mushroom decomposer", a "smell of death researcher", a "post-mortem jewellery designer" and a "morbid cake maker".[22] It might look like The Order of the Good Death is saying that we need to embrace death rather than be delivered from it, but this is still a deliverance. In their view deliverance is found in "accepting that death itself is natural, but [that] the death anxiety of modern culture is not".

Death is the final confirmation of our sneaking suspicion that all is not right in the world. While we may not be able to agree on the problem, let alone the solution, the principle upon which we can almost universally agree is this: we sure need saving from something. The question that occupies so much of our culture—our news bulletins, films and conversations with friends—is, how?

6. DESTINY
A Way to Control?

The camera focuses on a teenage girl standing on the stage waiting for the backing track to start. Her grandparents wait nervously in the wings. The viewer has already seen a little video montage of the girl filmed at her home (*accompanied by mournful tinkling piano music in a minor key*). She's come from a tough background and she's had a tough year. But she's strong (*swelling orchestral music comes now and changes to the major key*), and she's determined to make it—and make a new life for herself in the process. She's been told that she has a gift to share with the world and that she mustn't waste it. There have been so many obstacles to overcome; life has been against her, but here she is now on this stage. This is her chance. This is her moment. This is when it all changes...

"Why have you entered *Wanna Be a Star?* darling?" says one of the judges, chewing gum vociferously.

"Everything in my life has been leading to this," says our girl in a whisper.

She pauses. "I think I'm meant to be here."

Another pause. "I know I'm meant to be here."

Cut to the audience who have gone silent, with a camera picking up a woman clutching her partner and mouthing silently to him, "Oh, bless".

The music starts and our girl puts the microphone to her mouth...

30 seconds later, loud buzzers go off. It obviously wasn't meant to be...

Who's Writing the Script?

It's an unwritten rule that if you are a parent it's neither good nor healthy to have a favourite child. Well, I'm going to be honest with you—when it comes to the magnetic points, I have a favourite and it's this fourth one. It's called destiny and it asks whether there is a way we can control our lives.

This point describes a tension that we often find unbearable. Although we know ourselves to be active players in the world, at the same time we have a nagging feeling that we are passive participants in somebody else's world. Our limbs move, our mouth opens, but are there invisible strings attached? As human beings, are we truly free, or are we being pinned down by something or someone? Life courses between action and fate. Sometimes we feel like actors on a stage, aware that though we act out our part, we are working from someone else's script. Here's Bavinck again:

"A person is only master of his or her life up to a certain point. A power exists that repeatedly reaches into a person's existence, that pushes him or her forward with compelling force, and from whose grip the person finds it impossible to struggle loose. Sometimes people can despair that they can lead their own life. Sometimes they gradually achieve the insight, in the school of

life's hard knocks, that it is more appropriate to say that they suffer or undergo events that develop in and around them." [23]

What a way to put it: we both "lead" and "undergo" our lives. Isn't that a description of so many people we know or how we ourselves feel? This magnetic point is about the need to be in control and yet knowing we are somehow captive to events. It's about freedom versus fate.

Examples of Destiny

Throughout the history of philosophy and the great world religions, this tension has been evidenced in the most sublime and sophisticated ways. I could easily reference a Greek tragedy, or discuss the concepts of *qadar* in Islam or *karma* in Hinduism. Maybe I could impress you with a memorised quotation from a philosopher like Baruch Spinoza or a poet like Friedrich Schiller.

However, let's get real. Let's get inside the world of an average person in the 21st-century West. [24] Here's an example of destiny given to me by a student that captured my imagination:

"You must <u>never</u> say 'the phones are quiet' in the office. When I first started, I thought this was a bit of a joke, but it is considered deadly serious. You Do Not Say That. I've tried to talk it out with some colleagues, because they are clear that they have no belief in any sort of higher power, and are 'perfectly rational' people. At the same time, saying 'the phones are quiet' will result in (something/someone?) making said phones busy and unbearable. We simultaneously have no control over how our phone shifts are going to go ('you'll just have a day like that') and are responsible for our own/others' bad shifts ('because you said it was quiet and that made it busy'). There is a level of discomfort around breaking this rule that goes

beyond amusement, or social discomfort—it does result in real tension when someone 'curses' another person's shift. One of the interesting things about this power behind phone calls is that it is clearly malevolent. There's no good power responsible for quiet shifts or pleasant customers, just bad ones."

I thought this example might be a one-off, but I was wrong. A student who was an ex-policeman immediately confirmed that this really was "a thing". And then the floodgates seemed to open. Even a cursory internet search started to unearth what can only be called a "Quiet" conspiracy that I needed to investigate. Working day and night, I started to pin reports and photos on my wall, scribbling notes and highlighting dates, times and connections in red... Ok, I didn't really do any of that, but I did keep a lot of tabs open on my browser.

What I found was that professionals in many different fields observe this perplexing phenomenon. A local news reporter who joined a police patrol one New Year's Eve wrote:

"The unwritten rule of policing is that you never, ever, ever say it's 'quiet'. It is the curse of all curses which just invites trouble. It's like saying Macbeth on stage among a group of superstitious luvvies. [Instead] I post a tweet saying it's 'too "q"'. I so want to tempt fate but am aware that one of the officers in the van is 'monitoring' my tweets." [25]

A blogging doctor notes:

"'Wow, it sure is quiet today.' No phrase is more likely to strike terror in the heart of a physician than that innocent comment, made by a patient, a nurse, or, even worse, another physician. Saying a shift is 'quiet' is believed by many in health care to be the surest way to bring destruction on your head. Most patients don't know it, but there is no breed of human more superstitious

than a doctor doing shift-work. Perhaps it is the randomness of being on-call. Some days are an out-of-control, taking the corners-on-two-wheels disaster, narrowly avoiding endless crisis after crisis like a really bad computer game where no one gets extra lives. In contrast, some days are... well, let's not use the Q word." [26]

"Interesting," you may say, "Maybe 'Q' is 'a thing', but this is pretty superficial detective work, let alone proper research". But wait. The plot thickens. In my quest for truth I stumbled upon a co-authored research paper from *The Bulletin of the Royal College of Surgeons* at the beginning of April 2017 entitled, "Does the Word 'Quiet' Really Make Things Busier?"[27] This study claims to "make important developments in the field of superstition within modern medicine". Noting that due to under-staffing, National Health Service staff are the most stressed in any public sector, and so are always looking to reduce workload, "natural intrigue often leads hospital staff to use superstitious reasoning to infer meaning in situations we do not truly understand". The study deploys a multicentre, single blind, randomised control trial where at the end of a handover meeting one doctor would say, "Have a quiet night" and another would say, "Have a good night". After analysing the results, the authors state:

"This study has shown that when the word 'quiet' was used, a significantly higher number of admissions occurred during a night on-call period. It is the first of its kind to demonstrate a cost neutral, clinician-focused method of reducing workload in hospital. One can also conclude that avoiding the word 'quiet' may even reduce the incidence of traumatic injuries and orthopaedic emergencies within a hospital catchment area. The mechanism by which using the word 'quiet' causes an increase in workload is unclear. It is likely that the supernatural

forces at work are beyond the grasp of even the most skilled orthopaedic researchers. It is possible that such mechanisms might entail mythical microparticles such as 'interleukins' and 'prions', which may or may not exist in the real world. The ability to test such particles on the vast array of hospital investigations available has been noted but this testing has been avoided to prevent confusion. The true mechanism for our findings requires further work."

While cautioning against other superstitious practices ("covering yourself in bird poo, carrying a rabbit's foot on your lanyard or taping your fingers crossed"), when it comes to "Q" they make a number of recommendations, which include: senior management re-enforcing to staff that saying "Q" will make things busier; "the appointment of a 'Q' word specialist manager to oversee implementation of a 'Q' word eradication policy"; and the establishment of a nationwide public health initiative "to reduce the use of the word quiet in the public domain". They even proffer a ritual for reversing the effects of "Q" if said in error, based on the "cure" when an actor says "Macbeth": "the effect can be negated if the individual turns three times and utters certain incantations".

Now at this point, and before you contact The Good Book Company to say that Dr Strange has finally lost the plot, I recognise that this has all the makings of an elaborate and brilliant spoof. Yes, I too spotted the date of publication of the article (April 2017). However, in my defence, I've sent this paper round to a number of medical professionals and while the majority seemed to think it was a spoof, they were not completely sure. One believed it wasn't a spoof but simply dodgy research. Most importantly, for the purposes of this chapter, *all* recognised the Q-thing.

It's not just emergency and medical services where we see the magnetic point of destiny. Sport is a well-known breeding ground for these kinds of ideas.[28] Former Tottenham Hotspur Football Club manager Mauricio Pochettino has been open about his belief since childhood in "energía universal", described by one journalist as...

"... a sort of aura that powers the world and everyone and everything in it. People have an energy, but so do places, and so do moments and situations. 'Decisions, personal relationships and absolutely everything else are a matter of energy,' [Pochettino] writes in his book 'Brave New World'. 'Since those early days, I've had the ability to notice something powerful that you can't see, but does exist.'" [29]

Another article quotes him as saying:

"I believe in energía universal ... It is connected. Nothing happens for causality. It is always a consequence [of something else]. Maybe, it is one of the reasons that Harry [Kane] always scores in derbies. I believe in that energy. For me, it exists." [30]

Think of the amount of sophisticated sports science, minute planning and detail, and massive amounts of money and personnel that go into the running of a top-flight professional sports club. Then consider that Pochettino kept a bowl of lemons in his office because he believed that they absorbed negative energy from the room and that every three or four days he had to change them because they became ugly. This juxtaposition, in full view of the public and media, is striking.

However, even at a more normal and mundane level, "destiny" is there. People in our culture increasingly see their purpose in life as making the world a better place. But since, as I'm sure you've noticed, making a meaningful impact on the wider world is actually quite hard to achieve, more people seek to exert a greater degree of control in the smaller-scales areas in their life—diet, personal fitness, home interiors, leisure time and so on. In this sense, they can become to a certain extent fulfilled on the "micro level", and yet are ultimately dissatisfied by the ever-receding horizon of their goals on the "macro level".

In the 21st century we're constantly being told that we can do whatever we want and be whomever we want. I've heard it expressed like this: in the past, the call was for us to "Know thyself". Then in the 1980s and 90s the motto became "Be yourself" (remember the Spice Girls and "girl power"?). Today, it's "Define yourself". But even when this idea is embraced and promoted, we often still feel powerless and trapped. What about those people who decide they're going to get married at a certain point in their lives but then don't find a partner? Likewise with having children. Or consider the midlife crisis: it's essentially about the disappointment of not being what you'd wanted and losing that youthful sense that the future is your oyster. And then there's work. Working, working, working–but what's the actual point? Am I just treading water against the tide? What have I actually achieved in my life?

Or consider something like the housing market, where people feel powerless to "get on the ladder" because of larger controlling forces. The same could be said about our class, gender or ethnicity—often we feel locked in by our lot in life and don't see a way of escape. There is increased talk of impersonal "forces" (political, economic, environmental) that influence events, which gives the impression that individuals or groups have no responsibility, but also no agency. As a result, we are reduced to an entirely passive, anxious state: what's the next thing that's going to be done to us?

These tensions are all over our popular culture. The film *The Help* explores the characters' places in the world with regards to their racial identity, and how that does or doesn't control you. Viola Davis stars as an African-American domestic maid in 1960s Mississippi. The mantra that she repeats to the young (white) girl she looks after hints at the theme of destiny: "You is kind. You is smart. You is important". On the one hand it's communicating that need to be in control of our own destiny. On the other hand it's a recognition of the struggle that it is.

I think it's the irresistible power of destiny that explains our fascination with semi-scientific solutions that promise to "explain" us and give us a prophet-like knowledge of the future. Personality tests claim to illuminate why we behave like we do—suggesting that our behaviour and tastes are bound by our "type". 23andMe is a DNA kit you can use at home and which will tell you your likelihood of developing any number of diseases in the future.

My sister did one of these "Know your Ancestry" type tests. Apparently, as well as my mum's original Scandinavian heritage (although she was born and bred in Yorkshire, England), and my dad being Indo-Guyanese (so South Asian heritage), I'm also 1.9% Ashkenazi Jew and 2.9% Nigerian. The question is: how significant is this new information in explaining who I am, where I am and what I do?

A lot of best-selling psychology books that we might see people reading on the daily commute appear to challenge the "you're free to be who you want to be" narrative. We've already encountered *The Chimp Paradox*, which argues that we both lead and are led by our own brain. Inside us is something—our inner Chimp—which takes over our emotions, giving the sense that things happen to us and not because of us. But the tension of *The Chimp Paradox* is this: only the brain can control the brain. We are responsible for it in the same way as we are for a child or a dog. Similar ideas are found in Jonathan Haidt's *The Happiness Hypothesis*, where we are governed by our "elephants" (our unconscious mind), rather than our "riders" (our conscious mind).[31] Or are we even more determined? According to *The Self Illusion: Why There Is No 'You' Inside Your Head* by Bruce Hood, we are the product of implicit, automatic and unrelated microprocesses, which our brain constructs into the illusion of a "self" with its own story.[32]

So are we active players in the world? Or are we merely avatars moving under the thumbs of someone or something else? We feel like it's both—but how can that be? Those are the questions jostling around the magnetic point of destiny.

7. HIGHER POWER
A Way Beyond?

We're coming to the last stop in our tour of the magnetic points. The fifth and final point is what we might call the "super" magnetic point, or, depending on where you come from, the "Godfather", the "Daddy", or indeed the "Mother" of the magnetic points. Before we describe this final point we need to step back a few paces and give ourselves a bit of a run-up.

As we've looked at the magnetic points of totality, norm, deliverance and destiny, I hope you've noticed that these magnetic points are not totally distinct from each other but are linked together in various ways, with one overlapping with and implying another. Indeed, many of the examples I've given could be used to illustrate more than one point (remember *The Chimp Paradox* for both deliverance and destiny?). If you are someone who likes looking for patterns and connections, you might have paired together totality and destiny on the one hand, and norm and deliverance on the other. The reason for this goes back to what I said in chapter 3 about the origin of the magnetic points.

Remember, our magnetic points are what is left after human beings have suppressed and idolatrously substituted the knowledge of God in creation. God's invisible qualities have been clearly seen, so we are without excuse (Romans 1 v 20). We may twist and distort this revelation, but the "raw ingredient" that our suppression and substitution starts with is always revealed truth.

It's a bit like one of those police procedural programmes, where at the scene of an arson the fire investigator rummages around the smouldering wreckage to find the point of origin of the house fire. In the same way, as we tear away and sift through our damaged response to God (seen through the magnetic points), we reveal our point of origin: the revelation of God's eternal power, *implying human dependency*, and God's divine nature, *implying human accountability* (Romans 1 v 20). Totality and destiny "fit" with issues surrounding dependence: our smallness, our insignificance and our inability to do otherwise. Norm and deliverance "fit" with issues surrounding accountability: they recognise that we *can* do otherwise, that we *do* have responsibility, that we are individuals who have significance and that we can make a difference.

If we were in a good and healthy relationship with God, like Adam and Eve before the Fall, then dependence and accountability would fit together in perfect harmony, because God would be in the picture making sense of it all. But now things have gone haywire and there is a grating dissonance as we struggle with issues of dependence and accountability having pushed God out of the equation and replaced him with other things that act as God-substitutes. It's all a mess.

From Genesis 3 and onwards throughout human history, the more we are attracted by the magnetic points and the cultural fruit they produce, the more we recognise the complexity and seeming contradictions they present, and the more inquisitive we become. And as we enter further into the rabbit-holes of totality and destiny, of norm and deliverance, they all converge and land on our fifth and final magnetic point. Bavinck puts it like this:

"At the intersection of these two lines of thoughts—destiny within a totality and freedom to act and be delivered—lies the awareness of being related to a higher power. The higher power is at the same time the deepest meaning of the whole, the bearer of cosmic laws, the energiser of the norm, the helper toward salvation. That intersection of these two ones is obviously the heart of religious consciousness. Precisely there is where the unfathomable mystery of being human lies. Precisely there we find the essence of all religion." [33]

The fifth and final point is called higher power. It asks whether there is *a way beyond* the realm of our normal experience—a way to connect with someone or something higher than ourselves. Another word for this is transcendence.

On some level, all of us perceive that behind our reality stands a greater reality. This greater reality is variously conceived but is always a superior power. There is also a sense that humans stand in some sort of relationship to this higher power, or at least, that they should. This understanding creates the expressed desire to seek connection with this power—but what is it? Who is it?

Secular and Spiritual

Now, I want to be careful in my description of this final magnetic point. When our main man Bavinck was originally describing these points, he had very much in view what we would call "established religious traditions", all of which imagine a higher power. For example, in Islam it is a belief in

Allah; and in what we in the West have labelled "Hinduism", there are thousands, maybe millions, of personal gods, spirits and demons. In other instances, the higher power is believed to be more impersonal, like the concept of Brahman (again in Hinduism), the Ultimate Reality. In all of these examples, the notion of a higher power is quite close to the surface and doesn't require too much digging. So if you are reading this book in one of the many areas in the world where your neighbours include Muslims, Hindus, Sikhs, Buddhists or people of any number of other faiths, my telling you that all cultures exhibit a belief in a higher power is not going to be telling you anything new.

But there are millions of people who are *not* part of these traditions, and who wouldn't call themselves anything really. We normally describe them as secular. Does this final magnetic point apply to them? I think it does. In fact, given everything I've said so far about human beings, *it has to*. But there are some subtleties to bear in mind if we are going to get traction with this magnetic point. We're going to have to dig and it's going to be a bit harder work.

First, what does it mean to be "religious" or "secular"? In academic circles there are many competing theories and this question is a subject of quite a few sociological fist fights.

In the red corner are scholars who think that in the West, and for a whole load of complicated reasons I can't get into now, we have become immune to deep, religious experiences, being only in tune with what we might call "scientism" (the worldview which says that genuine knowledge of reality must be determined by the "hard" sciences of physics, chemistry, biology).[34] It's our John Lennon "above us, only sky" explanation of the world. I'm sure you know people who fit this description. As a result, these scholars argue that as a society we have become *disenchanted*.[35]

In the blue corner are scholars who point to various studies and surveys to show that we are as "religious" as ever when it comes to belief in the supernatural: in ghosts, lucky charms, occult healers, wizards, fortune tellers and *huldufólk*. I'm sure you know people who fit this description too. As a result, these scholars argue that we are as *enchanted* as ever.[36]

Now these boxers both land some meaty blows on each other, but which view is right? Well, I think they are both right, and they are both wrong. And I promise that's not just a total cop-out.

I do think that in the West, since the period known as the Enlightenment in the 17th and 18th centuries, there have been seismic changes in the area of belief. The menu of beliefs that we have at our disposal has changed, and so have the conditions of what we count as "believable". Scientism *is* a powerful force and continues to do it's best to suffocate what we might call the supernatural. As a result, ideas of the spiritual, let alone a higher power, need a little more digging out.

But *they have been and will always be there* because that's the way we are made. As one scholar has said, "The secular is haunted".[37] I didn't find it surprising to read that in a National Survey of Religion, 55% of participants claimed they had been protected from harm by a guardian angel.

Similarly interesting is a study led by a number of scholars in British universities called *Understanding Unbelief: Across Disciplines and Across Cultures*, the interim findings of which were published in 2019.[38] The project has interviewed thousands of people who identify as atheists and agnostics in six countries:

Britain, the United States, Brazil, China, Denmark and Japan. Two of the key findings are relevant here:

"Unbelief in God doesn't necessarily entail unbelief in other supernatural phenomena. Atheists and (less so) agnostics exhibit lower levels of supernatural belief than do the wider populations. However, only minorities of atheists or agnostics in each of our countries appear to be thoroughgoing naturalists.

"Another common supposition—that of the purposeless unbeliever, lacking anything to ascribe ultimate meaning to the universe—also does not bear scrutiny. While atheists and agnostics are disproportionately likely to affirm that the universe is 'ultimately meaningless' in five of our countries, it still remains a minority view among unbelievers in all six countries."

As was the case with our first four magnetic points, we can see our religiosity popping up all over the place. We just need to be looking closely and in the right places.

So Western culture today is not "dis-enchanted" but "diff(erently)-enchanted". It may not be the case that people believe in "God" or "gods"—at least, certainly not a personal one. Instead, they may have a vague belief in some form of "spirituality" or an openness to transcendence, or feel a connection to people or nature that's more than the sum of its parts. Others may say that they *know* that there can't be a higher power, but recall with wistfulness a time in our society when lots of people *did* believe in one. Such people often wish we could live in a society like that again, just without the "god" bit. They can't quite close the door on religion completely shut, and there remains a dissatisfaction and restlessness. I'm sure you can think of people like this.

Let's look at some examples of the higher power magnetic point.

Examples of Higher Power

Some immediately obvious ones would be the preoccupation with the supernatural: occult practices, horoscopes, Ouija boards and mediums. A former student of mine, who is now a minister in Lancaster, England, sent me an article from his local newspaper which featured necromancer and communicator-with-the-dead Dubhlainn Earley and his shop Bell, Book and Candle. The journalist writes:

"One of the strangest items on sale is dirt from graves, which Dubhlainn said is a powerful tool for rituals.

"He said: 'I get the soil on the soloist, a full moon. I have to research the person I am taking it from, I have to make sure they are good.'

"Dubhlainn said he leaves money at the grave as an 'exchange' for the dirt. 'I give two silver coins and whiskey, as long as I feel right I can then dig down and take the dirt. The last one was almost four feet, two inches deep. I've got [dirt] from police officers, judges, people who have protected other people in life.'" [39]

Even if we don't practise black magic ourselves, TV and film ratings bear witness to the fact that we like to watch all kinds of stuff on fairy tales, angels, demonic possession and exorcisms— especially when we're feeling flat and disenchanted with real life. Cosmic drama is a booming industry.

Then there are those who perceive themselves to be spiritual. There's the drive for minimalism and the rise in popularity of people like Marie Kondo. Having been "enchanted with organizing since her childhood", Kondo helps people to declutter their houses and theirs lives, and to get back to the "purity" of being. On her website she notes:

"The first thing I do when I visit a client is to greet their home. I kneel formally on the floor in the center of the house—or where its vortex is—and address the home in my mind.

"After introducing myself—including my name and occupation—I ask for help in creating a space where its inhabitants can enjoy a happier life. Then I bow. It's a silent ritual that only takes about two minutes.

"I began this custom quite naturally based on the etiquette of entering Shinto shrines. There can be tense anticipation before tidying, and I've discovered that connecting with the home can profoundly improve the process.

"Tidying is an opportunity to express appreciation for your home and all it does for you. Create a dialogue with your space—thank it for protecting and nurturing you—especially if you're about to embark on a tidying marathon!" [40]

What we might consider more traditional religions also still have an appeal. Alain de Botton wrote his book *Religion for Atheists: A Non-believer's Guide to Uses of Religion* saying that the real relevance of religion is in its traditions. There does seem to be a renewed interest in religious tradition, literature and places, almost as if a connection with spiritual history is a connection with something more solid than the ever-changing shifting sands of the new morality. Now history has become our foundation.

What about secular people's "religious experiences"? This can happen in places of outstanding natural beauty but also in more traditional religious settings. The father of a friend of mine said he "felt" something when visiting the Holy Sepulchre in Jerusalem. In a similar vein, this is from internet comic writer (and total atheist) Jerry Holkins, describing his visit to the Vatican:

"They keep bodies in that place, remains of saints and so forth, honored by gigantic statues placed above their tombs. I can't describe how still it made me. There is a statue of a seated St. Peter whose stone foot has been worn completely smooth— it looks like a hoof—by a procession of human beings long beyond numbering. Even as a person who is not really down with this sort of thing, it had a very pronounced effect on me. It is beautiful, and you can appreciate it either because it's the house of God or because human beings of tremendous talent and passion created something immortal.

"There is a room divided from the rest of the church by a curtain and a guard that is reserved for prayer only. I went in because I was there and I might as well see it, and once through the curtain I was struck as though by a physical force to kneel. I've never done anything like this, Catholics have a special kind of bench they pray on, and it is not a position natural to me so I nearly lost my balance. Where do my arms go?

"I won't inflict the particulars of my prayer on you. I just needed to tell someone what happened." [41]

My favourite and peculiarly British illustration of this is the recent phenomenon of "champing". Without reading on, take a few seconds to see if you can guess what "champing" is...

Paying to camp overnight in historical churches = Champing™

As Loyd Grossman (yes, of *MasterChef* and pasta sauce fame), former chairman of The Churches Conservation Trust says, champing "gives people a wonderful opportunity to quietly and intimately experience some of the most beautiful and inspiring historic buildings in the entire country. It's a very, very special way to feel close to history, to get to feel close to the lives of people who have worked in and lived around and have contributed to these churches over the centuries."[42]

In one local news report on champing, a middle-class mother was interviewed. She said that she wanted herself and her children to champ so they could experience waking up in the morning with natural light streaming through the stained glass windows. Another champer champion mentioned the importance of champers respecting the consecrated status of these historic buildings. At this point in the footage, the journalist notices a large wooden plaque on the wall inscribed with the Ten Commandments:

Journalist: "So people who come here, you welcome anybody, but they've got to be quite well-behaved because there's the Ten Commandments on the wall."

Champer: "Well that's an original part of the church but as champers we always ask that people respect the building because it is still a consecrated building."

Journalist (peering at the plaque): "'Thou shalt not commit adultery.' So if people come here for a naughty weekend, it's only with their own wives and husbands!"

Champer (nervously): "You can't say that!" [They both laugh]

Pick the magnetic points out of that!

PART 2

The Magnetic Person

8. Joining the Dots

We've now finished our tour of the magnetic points; the points that human beings are, always have been, and always will be, irresistibly attracted to:

- Totality: is there a way to connect?

- Norm: is there a way to live?

- Deliverance: is there a way out?

- Destiny: is there a way we control?

- Higher power: is there a way beyond?

These points are all pieces of one gigantic puzzle that on the box shows the picture of "human existence". Everything we do in our lives is an attempt to make these pieces fit together. Or to put it another way, these points are five itches that we're always scratching, as we try to find some relief from the irritating questions we have about ourselves and our world.

And we've seen from the Bible that these points are the messy mix of what God's image-bearers have done with God's revelation of himself in all of creation. Our dealings with these points are the ways in which we suppress the truth and substitute God with all kinds of other created things, both in the real world and in the world of our imagination. And *wow*, are we creative in our suppressing and substituting.

However, try as hard as we might, we can never wriggle free from these points because we can't escape our human-being-ness. And so, we're drawn to the points again and again, and we suppress and substitute again and again. This dramatic dance is the story of our lives.

At this stage, it might be tempting to conclude that our lives are just on one big repeating loop—that in our cosmic game of hide-and-seek, we have hidden ourselves so well, and buried ourselves so deeply, that we can't be found. In which case, all that's left for me to do is to thank you for reading, encourage you to come again, point you in the direction of the exit (via the well-stocked Magnetic Points gift shop), and give up.

But God hasn't given up on us. Just as God called out to Adam and Eve in the garden, "Where are you?", as one Christian apologist puts it, "Jesus Christ too is calling to us, saying the same words. He too is searching behind the bushes and calling, 'Man—my brother and sister—where are you?'"[43]

In the words of Bavinck:

"In the darkness of human existence, where repressing and replacing focus their empty work day and night, only the proclamation of the gospel of Jesus Christ can bring light. Truth is found in him. This is the complete and living power for people, the power long repressed and rejected. Contained in his words is always something of the 'I was always with you, but you were not with me.' 'I am the Christ whom you have repressed.' 'I am the one with whom you have struggled and whom you have assaulted.' 'It is hard for you to kick against the [goads].'"[44]

As I said in chapter 2, God is not a good hider, but he's the best seeker: "For the Son of Man came to seek and to save the lost" (Luke 19 v 10).

The good news of Jesus Christ and him crucified shatters our false and hopeless stories. Meeting Jesus pulls us out of our dark and dead-end tunnels. It wakes us up from our nightmares. It turns us the right way up. It is a better story—indeed, the best story—because it's real and true. I'm sure you can testify to this in your own life or in the lives of other Christians you know.

But how does this happen? It's by God's sovereign initiative. It's *only* by God's Holy Spirit that dead human hearts can be made alive. It's him who unmasks the world's sin (John 16 v 8). But this work doesn't happen through some mystical osmosis. It happens through God's word, the Bible. And the Bible is by no means one-dimensional. It consists of all kinds of literary genres which speak to all kinds of people and cultures: narrative, song, lament, law and letter. In the same way, as we share the Bible, we do so in all kinds of ways, and appealing to the whole person and all their faculties. We pray, we proclaim, we persuade, we preach, we argue, we refute, we prove.

1 Peter 3 v 15 calls us "to give the reason for the hope that we have". Giving a reason for hope is not only rational (although it's not less than that)—it's also emotional and imaginative. And while the agent of transformation is the Holy Spirit, I don't think this means that we aren't to work hard in our witness. The way we communicate the message does matter. In other words, the reasons we give, the arguments we offer and the stories we tell can all be more effective or less effective; more winsome or less winsome; more plausible or less plausible; and ultimately, more magnetic or less magnetic.

DANIEL STRANGE

So how do we communicate the gospel in a way that is truly magnetic? That's the aim in view as we start joining all these dots together. By way of introduction to the next six chapters, I want to outline three principles which will underpin what we're doing in the remainder of this little book.

Subversive fulfilment

First, *the gospel of Jesus Christ does not bypass the magnetic points, but is the subversive fulfilment of the magnetic points.* Subversive fulfilment is a concept that I wrote about in my previous book *Plugged In*. Let me briefly summarise it again.

Subversive fulfilment sounds complicated but it's not. It describes how compared to the idolatrous stories that the world tells, the gospel both subverts and fulfils them at the same time.

It *subverts* in that it confronts, gets inside, unpicks and overthrows the world's stories. It turns the tables on us by forcing us to look at the world in a new way, because it shows the old ways to be useless and harmful. It demands that we turn away from our old way of thinking and put our faith in the better story of Christ crucified. However, the gospel *fulfils* in that it connects with our deepest longings and is shown worthy of our hopes and desires. The gospel is a call to exchange old hopes and desires for new and more attractive ones—*because these new ones are the originals from which our false stories are smudges and ripped fakes.*

So, when it comes to our five magnetic points, what I hope to show is how the gospel of Jesus both connects with and wonderfully answers these magnetic points—intellectually, emotionally, *holistically*—but with answers that confront *our* idolatrous wrong "answers". Gospel answers will always present

88

a challenge to us; they will always make painful demands of us and our lives. This is what happens when we turn "from idols to serve the living and true God" (1 Thessalonians 1 v 9). But he is always ultimately worth it.

The Magnetic Person

Second, *the gospel message is the subversive fulfilment of the magnetic points, but our hope is not in a "what" but in a "who"*. In Acts chapter 8 we read of the encounter between the apostle Philip and an Ethiopian eunuch. The Ethiopian had been reading from Isaiah 53 but didn't understand it. "The eunuch asked Philip, 'Tell me, please, who is the prophet talking about, himself or someone else?'"

In many of our modern Bible translations the next verse reads something like this:

> *Then Philip began with that very passage of Scripture and told him the good news about Jesus. (Acts 8 v 35, NIV)*

However, it's older translations that might be more accurate here:

> *Then Philip opened his mouth, and began at the same scripture, and preached unto him Jesus. (Acts 8 v 35, KJV)*

Philip literally "evangelised him Jesus". The point is this: Christians are in the business of offering other people a person. Our "good news" is not that we offer commodities or even things like forgiveness, justification and peace. Christians are in the business of offering people *the Lord Jesus*, and it is he who brings forgiveness and who gives peace. The more we focus on the person of Jesus, the more vibrant our personal conversations and public proclamations will be. We come as persons and offer to other persons the person of

Jesus Christ "clothed in his gospel", to use the Reformer John Calvin's phrase.[45]

My day job for the last 15 years has been teaching would-be gospel ministers about culture, worldview and apologetics. To be honest, it can get pretty nerdy. It involves studying worldviews and philosophy, and uses phrases such as "cultural liturgies" and "social imaginaries" and "plausibility structures". Those are all things I'm deeply passionate about. However, all this stuff is not about looking sophisticated, or winning an argument; it's simply about getting better at offering people the person of Jesus.

We offer Jesus. Therefore, as we talk to people about the magnetic points (probably, of course, without ever using that phrase), we want to show how Jesus is the subversive fulfilment of the questions they're wrestling with. He is the magnetic person that we present to people.

The killer question that Jesus himself asked while he was on earth remains *the* question 2,000 years later: "'But what about you?' he asked. 'Who do you say I am?'" (Mark 8 v 29). Our aim in evangelism is to bring people to the point where they hear Jesus ask that question of themselves.

Ap-pealing, Ap-palling? Let's Call the Whole Thing Ap-ologetics

Third, *in offering Jesus as the subversive fulfilment of the magnetic points, we demonstrate both his magnetic appeal and how appalling idolatry is.* These are two different steps, yet they happen simultaneously. As the Christian apologist Os Guinness is fond of saying, "Contrast is the mother of clarity".

We see this very neatly summarised in Proverbs 26 v 4-5, although you might have to read these two verses through a couple of times, as at first glance they seem a bit of a brain-buster!

Do not answer a fool according to his folly,
or you yourself will be just like him.

Answer a fool according to his folly,
or he will be wise in his own eyes.

These are not contradictory statements. Rather, they complement each other. On the one hand, verse 4 stresses how we must answer unbelief not from its own basis and authority but from the rock-like authority of God and his word. Not to do so would be foolish and being foolish isn't going to help anyone. At the same time, verse 5 stresses the need to contrast this rock-like authority with folly. We are to walk around in the shoes of unbelief for the sake of argument and show up its foolishness, demonstrating that in the end it's not built on solid rock but shifting sand.

When we offer Jesus, his magnetic appealing-ness shows up the appalling-ness of idolatry. The living water that Jesus offers us contrasts with our cracked cisterns (Jeremiah 2 v 13). The more we show people Jesus, the more—we pray, by God's Holy Spirit—they will see the bankruptcy of any alternative worldview. And the more they see the shortcomings of idolatry, the more beautiful Jesus is shown to be in contrast. For the sake of the unbeliever, and in love, we seek to deliberately pull in opposite directions—the appealing one way and the appalling the other—stretching and creating an ever-mounting tension which becomes unbearable. Remember what we've said previously about the unbeliever: they know and they don't know; they are running to and running from.

They already live with this tension. For their sakes, we need to magnify it.

Doing this will take a good deal of trust—not so much trust in God (which I'm taking for granted), but trust that the magnetic points operate in all humans, no matter who they are, where they come from, and however uninterested they say they are in "religious" stuff. God's revelation in Scripture tells us otherwise: *everyone* is religious; *everyone* is suppressing and substituting the truth about God. And so as we strap ourselves into the harness of the magnetic points and Jesus' subversive fulfilment of them, we trust this analysis won't fail us.

Although many of our friends and family who don't know Jesus, are just living their lives— and, in Isaiah's words, do not "stop to think" about their idolatry and its implications (Isaiah 44 v 19)—they can't escape the magnetic points because they don't cease to be human. Even if people don't consciously reflect on the questions the magnetic points raise, everything they do in their lives is an answer to them. And it's our job to show them this. We don't come as bringing "religion" to them. We come as those offering answers to questions *they are already answering*, offering an exchange for religious commitments *they already have*, and offering a way to mend a relationship with God *they are already in*.

Getting Practical

How do we do all this? In *Plugged In*, I offered four practical steps to engaging faithfully and fruitfully with culture, based on Paul's encounter with the pagan philosophers in Acts 17:

1. *Entering: Stepping into the world and listening to the story.*
   "For as I walked around and looked carefully at your objects of worship..." (v 23).

2. *Exploring: Searching for elements of grace and the idols attached to them.* "People of Athens! I see that in every way you are very religious. For as I walked around and looked carefully at your objects of worship, I even found an altar with this inscription: TO AN UNKNOWN GOD" (v 23).

3. *Exposing: Showing up the idols as destructive frauds.* "Therefore since we are God's offspring, we should not think that the divine being is like gold or silver or stone— an image made by human design and skill" (v 29).

4. *Evangelising: Showing off the gospel of Jesus Christ as subversive fulfilment.* "So you are ignorant of the very thing you worship—and this is what I am going to proclaim to you" (v 23).

The same stages apply when it comes to offering Jesus as the subversive fulfilment of the magnetic points. The good news is that we've already covered the first two stages in our description and illustration of the magnetic points in chapters 2 – 7. Chapters 9 – 13 will cover stages three and four.

One final thing to flag. We've said that when it comes to evangelism, we are persons offering other persons the person of Jesus; so let's not miss that the people we're engaging with are *people*. That means communicating holistically and humanely. It demands love for, patience with and a "bearing with" tolerance of the other, which in the current climate is so counter-cultural. It requires the skills of listening carefully and the slow building of trust. We need emotional intelligence to recognise how we hear and how we are heard.

The challenge of offering Jesus will drive us to our knees in prayer. But we pray in the confidence that because the Bible says we are God's image-bearers who know but who suppress and substitute the truth, we *will* discern the magnetic points in a person's life. We pray in the confidence that at some level—however deep we have to go, however hard they deny and hide—our friends are itching, restless, haunted, disappointed and despairing. And we pray in the confidence that we offer a Jesus who says, "Come to me, all you who are weary and burdened, and I will give you rest" (Matthew 11 v 28).

Offering Jesus in this way is not smooth or pain-free, but it is life-changing. In the words of Bavinck:

"The gospel of Christ addresses people and rips open their religiousness consciousness. People want to suppress and push away the gospel in the worst way, just as they have repeatedly done with God. But it can happen that God causes their heart to submit. Then all the engines of resistance are switched off and people listen. Then the King of Glory makes his entrance, the everlasting doors of the understanding are thrown open. And this is what we call the new birth." [46]

9. JESUS
The Way We Connect

The magnetic point called totality asked if there is a way for us to connect—with each other and with the world around us. It revealed a fundamental identity problem we have as human beings which makes us dizzy and confused. On the one hand, we want to champion our individuality—the big "I" which gives us a sense of significance and control. The problem is that this easily tips us into another big "I"—isolation—and leaves us with a sense of loneliness and insignificance. So we push the see-saw down at the other end and search for our identity by trying to connect to something bigger than ourselves, in order to give us a sense of meaning and purpose—a sense of totality. We want connection but *without* losing our individuality and freedom.

Yet these bigger things in some way always fall short of delivering a satisfying sense of totality. Let's revisit some of the examples I mentioned in chapter 3 to see how.

Sporting and music events are fun but don't last. You sing your heart out together at the stadium as if you are one huge, connected organism, but then you totally ignore each other on the bus on the way home. Remember my walk during lockdown and the posters I came across? We can talk a good game about connecting through *"Ubuntu*—I am because we are", or the solidarity of "being a Londoner" because we stand on the right of the escalator, but what's the *quality* of that connection?

The evidence suggests that it is not all that good. It feels as though we're told every week that loneliness is a massive problem and that rates of mental illness are rising. Over a quarter of the US population now live on their own, and studies suggest that the average American has fewer close friends now than they did a generation ago. British and American culture seems increasingly fragmented and tribalised with a loss of both common vision and community. In 2019 (*pre*-COVID!), it was reported that pubs were closing down in the UK at the rate of one every twelve hours.[47] Where do people actually meet each other these days? Longer working hours mean that many people have no time for community, but they don't have a community to go to anyway. Lots of us don't even know our neighbours, let alone love them. A friend of mine noted that they've lived in many flats where they've heard the feet of the people upstairs but would not have been able to recognise their faces. National events such as our response to COVID might have injected us with a sense of unity and togetherness in the UK, but it all wore off quickly. Before the end of the year we had descended into divisions over lockdown, Brexit and whether the United Kingdom should stay "united".

And what about those communities that have founded themselves on the principles of inclusion and a shared identity, such as the LGBT community? This has long been a home for those who feel marginalised and ostracised, yet it increasingly demonstrates internal conflicts, tensions and powerplays between the different "initials" (lesbian, gay, bisexual and trans). As the commentator Douglas Murray points out: "The L's don't need the G's today, and the G's don't much care for the L's and almost everybody can be united in suspicion of the B's. And there is tremendous dispute over whether the T's are the same thing as everybody else or an insult to them."[48]

But that's not the only example of the headaches caused when two identities and allegiances clash with each other. In June 2020 *Harry Potter* author J.K. Rowling tweeted a response to an article entitled "Opinion: Creating a more equal post-COVID-19 world for people who menstruate". Rowling wrote, "'People who menstruate.' I'm sure there used to be a word for those people. Someone help me out. Wumben? Wimpund? Woomud?" She followed the tweet with this comment, arguing for the importance of being able to use the word "woman": "If sex isn't real, there's no same-sex attraction. If sex isn't real, the lived reality of women globally is erased. I know and love trans people, but erasing the concept of sex removes the ability of many to meaningfully discuss their lives. It isn't hate to speak the truth."

This provoked a fierce backlash from some quarters, with people such as Mallory Rubin (Chief Editor of influential site *The Ringer*) tweeting at the time: "Harry Potter is about the magic of love, acceptance, belonging. The power of courage. The impact of hope. Trying to take those things away from people is a terrible tragedy. Trans women are women." The row raised the question of whether trans rights and women's rights are at odds with each other. And in case this all sounds like a proverbial storm in a tea cup, note that six months later, as I write this, the conversation continues, with the BBC recently airing a radio programme, *Seriously... Can I Still Read Harry Potter?* where non-binary journalist Aja Romano examines her decision to put down the books she has obsessed over for years because of Rowling's comments.[49] If we're looking for a sense of totality from our gender or sexual identity (or indeed, from our devotion to a fantasy fiction series), we'll soon be faced with inconsistencies.

And what about the search for "the one": that perfect romantic relationship, the person who will complete me and give me ultimate satisfaction and connection? Will that deliver a satisfying sense of totality? You've probably lived long enough in the real world to know that the answer to that question is no. We may never find such a person and so remain feeling "incomplete". Or, if we do think we have found that person, we may load so many expectations and dreams on them that when they frustrate us, disappoint us, and fail us, we conclude that this wasn't "the one" after all. We might decide it's time to disconnect and look for someone new, but such disconnection is often so costly, complicated and damaging. Commitment in human relationships is very good, but over-commitment leads to all kinds of problems. Romantic relationships in themselves can never deliver the sense of totality that we are wired for.

Totality Evangelised

So how does the gospel of Jesus Christ subversively fulfil this magnetic point of totality? And how do we start talking to our friends about it?

What follows in this chapter are the main points of the Christian story that I'm seeking to drop into my daily life and daily encounters; the kinds of things I'm trying to highlight as I go about chatting, discussing, preaching, writing, singing and creating. I realise this is my own personal take. You'll have your own creative ways of doing it. And it's also fair to say that communicating this all at once is a bit like a hosepipe down the throat—in real-life evangelism, more often the aim is to sprinkle little tastes of truth into conversation and see where it leads. But hopefully what follows will help you get the idea and will get you talking about this kind of stuff in your own contexts and relationships.

As I said in the last chapter, in our presentation of the gospel, our focus needs to be on offering a person—*the* magnetic person, Jesus Christ. The aim is to use our words to paint a compelling portrait of Jesus, and invite others to stop and look and consider him for themselves.

However, as any art-lover will tell you, great paintings need great frames. William Bailey from New York's Museum of Modern Art wrote a whole book on that very subject! He wrote that the frame and its design "must effect a transition from the existing physical location, usually a wall in a room or a gallery, into the illusionistic realm of the painting. This should occur graciously and imperceptibly. The frame should also prepare the eye and mind of the viewer to accept and embrace the domain of the painting on its own terms."[50] The right frame enhances the viewer's enjoyment of a painting; the wrong frame distracts from it.

We have a wonderful portrait of Jesus for people to view, and we want to make sure that we have the best frame around our portrait to show him off in all his splendour. In other words, we'll often need to give people the framework of a Christian worldview in order for Jesus' death and resurrection to make sense. This is essentially what we see Paul doing in Athens in Acts 17. As Paul preaches in the market-place, the Athenians who hear him are confused, calling him a "babbler", or more literally a "seed-picker": one who scavengers and pecks at ideas that don't fit together (v 18). So when Paul is hauled up to address the council at the Areopagus, his speech contains a *run-up* and a *run-through*. His run-up connects with the way that the Athenians already understand the world, and then his run-through lays out the basic building blocks of a Christian worldview in order that Jesus and the resurrection make sense. In our post-Christian context, where the Christian faith is so misunderstood, or even not known, I think we need to adopt a similar approach.

The Totality Frame-work

When we embrace the Christian teaching on being human, we find that we don't have to constantly flip-flop between our sense of insignificance and significance. The Bible's answer to the questions around totality is a beautiful and satisfying both-and, not an either-or. Let me put it like this:

- We are created *by* God (Genesis 1 v 26). This immediately implies one who is the source of our life, who has given us the gift of life.

- We are created *in* God's image (Genesis 1 v 26). Being made in God's image means two things. There is a sense in which we are insignificant because we are only *images* and not divine. But at the same time we have a unique significance—a sense of royalty, even—because we are images of God. We have genuine dignity but it's defined by us being creatures, not the Creator.

- We are created *from* the earth; that's what the name "Adam" means (Genesis 2 v 7). Therefore we can affirm our desire for connection with everything around us, and our affinity for the natural world, because we are part of it.

- We are created *for* relationships, not only with creation in general but with other human beings in particular (Genesis 2 v 18). Being alone is not our natural state and is not good for us. However, our relationships with creation and with other human beings only make sense in the context of our relationship with God—when they are regarded as gifts from him.

- We are created *with* a purpose—to make a home for ourselves *together*, using God's blueprint but with a God-given creativity (Genesis 1 v 26). As God's image-bearers we are speakers and makers, and we build culture(s) with others who share with us our ultimate loves and desires.

In summary, humans were created to be dependent, dignified, responsible and therefore also accountable. This is the frame of our story.

However, something has gone terribly wrong. Although we crave connection, we are disconnected in so many ways. We are disconnected from ourselves, in that we don't know who we are, or what makes "me", "me". Often we're at war inside our own heads and with our own bodies. We're disconnected from each other. Although we sometimes get a tantalizing taste of totality, we often feel that we are not meaningfully connected with each other, and instead feel misunderstood, alienated and alone. Whether it's as a child in the playground, or as an adult in the office, we all know that sickness in the pit of our stomachs when we realise that we're on the outside of that joke, not included in that trip to the pub, and just left out. Finally, and in a way that we are increasingly sensitive to, we're disconnected from our environment. We are in awe of the natural world yet at the same time acknowledge that we're making a mess of it; we are at a loss to know how best to steward the resources we've been given so that our species and our planet can both flourish.

These disconnects within us, around us and amongst us are the consequences of the biggest disconnect of all—we're disconnected from the one who made us. We've turned our backs, run from and hidden from the one who gave us life. We've told lies about the only one who speaks truth. In not wanting to face our Maker and his truth, we've put our hopes, dreams and fears in other things that don't deserve our worship and that can't give us the identity, meaning and communion we so long for. Desiring to be connected to this world is foolish and tragic because it means a connection to a world that is under judgment, that is cursed and perishing—for from dust we came and to dust we will return (Genesis 3 v 19). It's futile. And our disconnection from God will ultimately lead to an eternity spent in the "outer darkness" (Matthew 22 v 13, ESV).

Jesus: The Way We Connect

But let me offer you Jesus. There are so many rich ways that the Bible talks about who Jesus is and what he came to do. Jesus is the true image of God, the second Adam who walked on the earth 2,000 years ago and who both proclaimed and ushered in another reality—another world—with himself at the centre of it all.

But as regards the theme of totality, let's go all horticultural. Jesus said:

> I am the vine; you are the branches. If you remain in me and I in you, you will bear much fruit; apart from me you can do nothing. If you do not remain in me, you are like a branch that is thrown

away and withers; such branches are picked up, thrown into the fire and burned. (John 15 v 5-6)

In the Old Testament, the image of a fruitless vineyard had been used to describe the disobedient people of Israel; they were not the people they were called to be (Isaiah 5 v 4; Psalm 80). In saying he is "the vine", Jesus is saying that he is the true Vine—in his person and work he both subverts and fulfils the vine of Israel. Jesus flourishes and brings flourishing to others in the way that Israel failed to do.

But Jesus is also making a universal claim in these verses that is for all humanity to hear. He is the Vine—the life-giving source and centre—not simply for Israel but for everyone.

Being connected to the vine—being "in" it and staying attached to it—is how a branch flourishes and is fruitful. Cut it off and it ceases to be a branch; it becomes a dead stick. And Jesus says that the same is true of us and him. We "remain" in him by recognising our dependence on him, trusting his promises and throwing ourselves on his love—a love in which he lays down his life for his friends (John 15 v 13). As branches to a vine (literally, "vine to a vine"), we are connected to Jesus in the closest of ways, but without losing our individuality and responsibility (since it is still beholden on us to "remain in [him]"). Remaining in Christ means the end of our search for totality; it means rest from our restlessness. We *can* be part of something bigger—because we become part of *someone* bigger. And while this does involve surrendering our independence— in the words of the apostle Paul, "I have been crucified with Christ and I no longer live, but Christ lives in me" (Galatians 2 v 20)—we do so knowing that our so-called "independence" put us in the same condition as a branch lying on the ground unattached from the tree: namely, dead.

Our connection with Christ means we get an identity—his identity—but without isolation. Jesus knows us better than we know ourselves. He is always with us and always loves us, so no matter how disconnected we might feel in our lives and relationships, we can never say we are alone or that *no one* understands us. Jesus knows, Jesus understands, because he is one of us. We can come to him, at any time, from anywhere and in any circumstance. Jesus' connection with us is one of total and unbreakable solidarity and compassionate comfort. What a Saviour! What a friend!

Through Christ we enjoy connection and communion with God, but also connection and community with each other. After all, if I am connected to Jesus, and you are connected to Jesus, then in a very real way we are connected to one another. Listen to Jesus again in John 15 as he addresses his disciples:

> *As the Father has loved me, so have I loved you. Now remain in my love. If you keep my commands, you will remain in my love, just as I have kept my Father's commands and remain in his love. I have told you this so that my joy may be in you and that your joy may be complete. My command is this: love each other as I have loved you. (John 15 v 9-12)*

I'm convinced that the church has the opportunity to fill a massive gap in our secular and fragmented market. The sense of connection offered by the Saturday football match or the stadium concert are nothing compared to the sense of connection offered by genuine Christian fellowship. The church is far bigger in its global reach; far longer lasting in that it stretches back through the Old Testament and forward to eternity; and far deeper, stronger, and more permanent than any human association—because it's not a human association! It's God's new community. And it is expressed as we love one another in the context of the local church.

A genuine, diverse, loving, trustworthy church family is a big attraction for many today who long for community and inclusion but don't know where to find it. Here's how one friend tells it:

"This was key in my own conversion. I remember being 18 and having a deep philosophy that I really wanted to love everyone in the world and for everyone in the world to love me. I got converted going to a Christian camp where I found it for the first time. I distinctly remember Lance, a fat kid who had very low self-esteem, the kind of kid you knew was used to being picked on. But I saw the cool kids befriend him and how it made him smile. It was totally the opposite of my experience of school."

In his offer of identity, communion and community, Jesus Christ shows himself to be the subversive fulfilment of the magnetic point of totality. And so we extend this invitation to others: turn around and come to him.

10. JESUS
The Way We Live

The second magnetic point, norm, asked if there is a way to live. We know that there are standards and rules, and we also know that we *need* these standards and rules in place to be able to live our lives as individuals and as a community. We may well struggle with them, and struggle to live by them, but we can't live without them. We illustrated this magnetic point with all kinds of examples, from paper straws to work-appraisal systems and video assistant refereeing.

Even in the description of these examples, I hope you already started to see the legitimate questions that the norm raises, together with the many unsatisfactory answers that are forthcoming.

There are questions about the nature of the norm: Where do these rules come from? Who decides them? One person? One party? The majority? The minority? Where does our inner sense of "ought" come from? Is it simply a case of human customs and conventions that are socially constructed? Can we ever have rules and standards that are clear and obvious for everyone?

Then there are questions about living with the norm: How do I resolve my desire to express my individuality with my craving to fit in? And what happens when others break the rules or don't live up to these standards? Is there justice or injustice? Does deviation from the norm call for tolerance or intolerance? And what happens when *we* break the rules and don't live up to these standards? Do we feel guilty or ashamed? If not, why not? If we do feel guilty, then what, if anything, can we do about it? Is it really one strike and we're out?

The upshot of all this is that living with norm produces some pretty undesirable consequences. First, it's often a breeding ground for pride, hypocrisy, false humility and virtue signalling. We want to—no, we *need* to—feel good about ourselves by feeling "bad" about someone else. Second, and at the same time, living with norm is tiring. Being virtuous was hard enough, but now we have to be *seen* to be virtuous, and it's exhausting. Third, living with norm is anxiety-laden, as I'm fearful of falling foul of the standard myself and so having people judge me. Finally, living with the norm is also increasingly troubling in our supposedly "tolerant" society, because when it comes to rule-making, harsh and arbitrary rules are the definition of another word beginning with the letter "T": tyranny. The late philosopher Roger Scruton was sacked as chairman for a government commission after making remarks in an interview that were deemed offensive. In an article entitled "An apology for thinking", he commented:

"We in Britain are entering a dangerous social condition in which the direct expression of opinions that conflict—or merely seem to conflict—with a narrow set of orthodoxies is instantly punished by a band of self-appointed vigilantes. We are being cowed into abject conformity around a dubious set of official doctrines and told to adopt a world view that we cannot examine for fear of being publicly humiliated by the censors. This world view might *lead to a new and liberated social order; or it might lead to the social and spiritual destruction of our country. How shall we know, if we are too afraid to discuss it?"*[51]

So how does the gospel of Jesus Christ subversively fulfil this magnetic point of norm? Here are the main points of the Christian story to highlight in our frame-work and our portrait of Jesus.

The Norm Frame-work

Once again, we begin with creation and our being made in the image of God. As image-bearers we were not designed to make up our own rules for living; we were built to be dependent on God for this knowledge. It's by doing things his way that we will not simply survive but thrive. As we see in any of our favourite TV cookery shows, closely following the maker's instructions leads to the best results. Not only are we dependent but we are dignified by having responsibility for ourselves and our actions. Being responsible means we will be held accountable if we don't follow these inbuilt instructions.

Tragically, we've gone rogue. We've decided to follow our own script and make our own rules. But we can never escape our need for a standard and a sense of accountability, even if it's only to ourselves. It's hard-wired into us. You can call it a conscience if you like. Sometimes it accuses us, sometimes it defends us, sometimes it's way off the mark, but it's always there. We can try and ignore it or explain it away but our explanations never quite account for it. It's this hard-wiring that explains where our internal sense of "ought" comes from—why we feel like our life and our world *ought* to be different. It's the reason that although we struggle to define justice, we know we want it, and we burn when we experience injustice.

And however sensitized or de-sensitized our conscience might be, however much we try to hide, however twisty and turny we make our excuses, as dependent creatures, at some level we know we've committed the ultimate case of "biting the hand that feeds us". We remain responsible and accountable and the shame and guilt this produces is always lurking in the depths of our souls. And the Bible says that the justice we want to see will come right back at us; the consequences of breaking the Creator's norm will be realised by a God who only deals in right judgments.

Jesus: The Way We Live

But let me offer you Jesus:

> I am the way and the truth and the life. No one comes to the Father except through me. (John 14 v 6)

When it comes to the norm, Jesus doesn't just reveal that there is a standard, he says, *I am the standard.* Jesus doesn't throw away the rule book, he *is* the rule book. Jesus doesn't carry a set of rolled up blueprints under his arm, he *is* the blueprint. The norm of which we are aware, even if only faintly, is not a set of dry, abstract and impersonal rules but is embodied in a magnetic person. Everything that God had revealed in the Old Testament about what makes for human flourishing and for *shalom* (peace) in our communities was fully realised in Jesus' teaching and in his person. Jesus said, "Do not think that I have come to abolish the Law or the Prophets; I have not come to abolish them but to fulfil them" (Matthew 5 v 17). He summed up quite simply what the norm is:

> "Love the Lord your God with all your heart and with all your soul and with all your mind." This is the first and greatest

commandment. And the second is like it: "Love your neighbour as yourself." All the Law and the Prophets hang on these two commandments. (Matthew 22 v 37-40)

As Jesus reveals God's norm, he calls himself "the way and the truth and the life" (John 14 v 6). The "way" is not simply about an entry point to get in, or a destination point to get to, but a way to follow. Jesus gives us a "way of life".

To say, "I am the way" is a big claim. So what gives Jesus the authority to set that standard? Why should we listen?

Just think for a minute. We all have authorities in our lives and we regard them with differing levels of importance, trust and obedience, based on at least three questions. First, do they have the knowledge? Do they have the facts and can they interpret those facts correctly? If we thought the Chancellor of the Exchequer/Secretary of the Treasury knew nothing about economics and finance, we would be worried. Second, what about their ethical character? Do we trust them? Do they have integrity? If it's a person, have they kept their promises in the past? Third, are they effective? Does what they say is going to happen, happen? Do their words have the power not simply to describe reality but also to shape reality?

All of these three things have to be in place in order for someone to have our trust, respect and obedience. Someone can have all the knowledge but be totally ineffective. Someone can get things done but be taking the wrong course of action entirely. Someone can have great integrity but not know what they're talking about.

When we meet the person of Jesus we see someone who demonstrates these three things perfectly. He knows all things, because through him all things were created and in him all things hold together (Colossians 1 v 16). He has perfect knowledge of us and of our future.

He is totally trustworthy; he does not lie. He looks after others, not himself. While he was on earth he demonstrated love, compassion and servant-heartedness without fail, even though he was the rightful King of all those he served. And Jesus is kind; one of the reasons he turned water into wine at a wedding he attended was because he didn't want the bridegroom to suffer the public humiliation of having to tell his guests that the wine had run out (John 2). What a lovely gesture. And think of all those healings and miracles he performed. When a lady who had internal bleeding reached out to him in desperation, Jesus spoke tenderly to her; when the daughter of Jairus got sick and died, Jesus raised her and reunited her with her parents; when hungry crowds gathered around him, Jesus fed them. And there was never any posturing or virtue signalling of any kind. Jesus is not showy; he truly is gentle and humble in heart.

Jesus' words are always effective. When there was a terrible storm and his disciples thought they were going to drown, Jesus told the wind and waves to be quiet, and they were. He called his dead friend Lazarus to come out of his tomb, and he did. He said he would be killed and rise again three days later, and it happened.

As an authority, indeed *the* authority, Jesus is to be trusted. He doesn't make us choose between either rules or relationship, or between love and obedience. In our culture, these are pitted against each other, but in Jesus they are in harmony. He is worthy of both our love and our obedience.

In this way, Jesus is *the* norm who both subverts and fulfils *our* norms, whatever our views on the 21st-century's changing moral order. He challenges and appeases the two squabbling siblings that are prevalent in our secular morality: conservatism and liberalism. I know I'm generalising, but here's what I mean.

On the one hand, you have "the conservatives". Perhaps such people would be associated more to the right of the political spectrum. These conservatives are fearful of moral change and so stand against these changes (with regards, for example, to sexuality and gender). The gospel appeal for these people is that Jesus never changes; he is the same "yesterday and today and for ever" (Hebrews 13 v 8). His morality is solid, dependable and really "real". The gospel challenge for these types of people is that Jesus asks hard questions about the motivation behind their call for the status quo. Is it more about a self-righteous pride and judgmentalism and the need to look down on others so we feel good about ourselves than it is about a love of our neighbour? Isn't it really our own insecurities and fears that is at the root of our cries to conserve?

On the other hand, you have the more liberal, "progressives". They want to change the moral order. Superficially they appear to be against Christianity and are challenged and even offended by Jesus' clear teaching in many areas. However, their deeper motivations are often good ones. They want to help the marginalised, the poor and those who are victims. They are passionate advocates for those who feel trapped, scared and unable to say anything. The gospel appeal for such people is the way that, time and again in the Gospels, we see how Jesus had compassion for the outcast and the courage to stand against the conservatives of his day who were only interested in rules for rules' sake. They might assume that Jesus is conservative, but in this sense Jesus was the very opposite because, once again, his morality is real and deep and is about a change of heart.

Jesus is indeed *the* norm and *the* standard. However, the standard that Jesus sets is higher than any standard we set for ourselves. Jesus told us that human beings are to love the God who made us with all our heart and with all our soul and with all our minds, and to love our neighbour as ourselves. The elephant in the room is that we haven't done that—indeed, we've done the opposite. We've rebelled against the God who made us, rejected him and his blueprint for life, and we now treat our fellow image-bearers in ways which denigrate their humanity. And when God sent his Son into the world, we rejected him too. We're guilty as charged.

Jesus says that your sense that the world is not as it should be is precisely right—*and you can't fix it.* This was beautifully expressed by Queen Elizabeth herself in her Christmas Day speech in 2011:

"Although we are capable of great acts of kindness, history teaches us that we sometimes need saving from ourselves—from our recklessness or our greed. God sent into the world a unique person—neither a philosopher nor a general, important though they are, but a Saviour, with the power to forgive."

The amazing good news is that Jesus is not only the *standard* but he is also the *Saviour* who takes the initiative for a helpless human race. For every day of his earthly life, Jesus loved God with all his heart, soul and strength and loved his neighbour as himself. He kept God's law perfectly. And when men and women come to Jesus, his obedience is accounted to us. We are clothed in his perfection as if it were our own. And we are given God's Spirit, who begins a work in us to make us every day more like the Jesus we follow and love. The follower of Jesus does not say, "I obey so I'm accepted", but rather "I'm accepted so I obey". When it comes to the norm, the Christian can never be proud in anything they have done for themselves. It's not about us, it's about Jesus.

Remember those horrible consequences of the norm? Trying to keep our own norms only breeds hypocrisy, but embracing Jesus as the way to live will foster humility. Instead of being plagued by anxiety and guilt when we fail to live up to the standard, in Christ we can rejoice in grace and experience a liberating forgiveness for all our failures. And with Jesus we no longer need to suffer the exhaustion of being obsessed with ourselves and how others think of us. Instead, we can focus on others, look out for them and serve them. And because Jesus is the standard and the one who is the perfect authority over us, we no longer have to live in fear of tyranny of any kind— we need not be oppressed by anyone else's expectations. Jesus says: "Come to me, all you who are weary and burdened, and I will give you rest. Take my yoke upon you and learn from me, for I am gentle and humble in heart, and you will find rest for your souls" (Matthew 11 v 28-30).

And unlike that static work-appraisal system, God's work in us to make us more like Jesus is not like a cookie cutter producing Christian clones. Certainly, God's norms remain unchanging, but our individuality and distinctiveness is respected. We all start our journey with Jesus from different places, and we grow at different paces, but every Christian is growing nonetheless. Although it's great to have role models and be encouraged by others, we don't have to play (and lose) a godliness comparison game.

Jesus is the standard we all want, and Jesus is the Saviour we all need. But here's the thing: *you can't have one without the other.*

This point is especially important in our particular cultural moment. When it comes to Jesus as the norm, we are not only talking about a standard for personal piety and personal living, but for culture and society. Historically, it has been God's word, the Bible, which has influenced our Western culture and that has produced the norms that we cherish most deeply—values such as equality, kindness and mercy. This needs to be remembered and celebrated.

Christianity's historic influence is illustrated by the fact that in the coronation service for Queen Elizabeth II in 1953, the queen was presented with a Bible and these words:

"Our gracious Queen: to keep your Majesty ever mindful of the Law and the Gospel of God as the Rule for the whole life and government of Christian Princes, we present you with this Book, the most valuable thing that this world affords. Here is Wisdom; this is the royal Law; these are the lively Oracles of God."

Almost 70 years on, although the water is quickly running out of the bath, our Western culture still lives off the capital of a Christian worldview. Our culture's norms and conventions are still related to Jesus' norms written in the Bible, but with a diminishing view of our need for the cross. When you try to have a culture shaped by a Christian standard but without a Christian Saviour, you end up with the confusion we described in chapter 4.

But it would be a mistake to suggest that this hasn't always been a danger. William Wilberforce, the leader of the movement to abolish the slave trade, wrote about what he saw as the decline of Christianity in the 18th century:

"The fatal habit of considering Christian morals as distinct from Christian doctrines insensibly gained strength. Thus the peculiar doctrines of Christianity went more and more out of sight, and as might naturally have been expected, the moral

system itself also began to wither and decay, being robbed of that which should have supplied it with life and nutriment."[52]

Wilberforce is saying that you can't have the moral fruit of Christianity without the root—those "peculiar doctrines" of Christianity that make the gospel what it is: our need for a Saviour; our need for the God-man Jesus Christ. Without this root, the fruit will die.

But with this root—with Jesus as both our standard and Saviour—we can enjoy a life of freedom and flourishing. Jesus Christ shows himself to be the subversive fulfilment of the magnetic point of norm. So we invite people to turn around and come to him.

11. JESUS
The Way Out

Our third magnetic point asked whether there is a way out, or even, a way back to what we've lost. Deliverance can show itself either in us looking back in longing or looking forward in hope. Whether it's in our lives, in our society, or on a global scale, we know that things are broken and need fixing. We spend our time, energy and money trying to work out what our greatest problem is so that we can administer the most effective solution which will give us the world we all want. The problem is that we don't agree on what holds us back and keeps us in chains, let alone how we might escape and be set free.

And even if we *did* agree, the question we must pose is: will our "deliverances" actually deliver? Two decades ago British Prime Minister Tony Blair pledged that his priority was going to be "education, education, education", and successive governments since have promised something similar—but where is the societal enlightenment that we thought would result? When we look at politics on both sides of the Atlantic in recent years—whether it's this policy or that policy, this leader or that leader, this administration or that administration—it's hard to claim that any of them have had any significant success in improving social unity and cohesion. Indeed, as a culture we seem more fragmented, fractured and fragile than ever.

Sometimes we're willing to recognise the failure of our deliverances. In 1997, and a day after the death of Princess Diana, rock band The Verve released *The Drugs Don't Work*, an anthem that always gets a high ranking in various "Best of" music charts. At the time it was written, its composer Richard Ashcroft was interviewed:

"'There's a new track I've just written,' he says, nervously avoiding eye contact. 'It goes "the drugs don't work, they just make me worse, and I know I'll see your face again". That's how I'm feeling at the moment. They make me worse, man. But I still take 'em. Out of boredom and frustration you turn to something else to escape.'" [53]

If substances can't save us, what about music itself? I've already referenced the BBC interview with the classical pianist Murray Perahia whose upbringing was within an orthodox Sephardic Jewish family. Towards the end of that interview Perahia was asked what music could do to improve the world. He answers:

"I'm very pessimistic ... that it will really have an impact because there's a very interesting dichotomy in music. You're changed as a person while you are listening to music but when you're not listening to the music anymore you become the same person you were five minutes before. And it's a myth to think that musicians are any nicer or deeper or more human than anybody else. I mean a case in point was Cortot [Alfred Cortot, one of Perahia's musical heroes] who was not a very nice man and betrayed a lot

of Jews to the Nazis, and was one of the greatest pianists that ever lived." [54]

I think Perahia is onto something here. Call me a cynic, but I'm afraid that a stadium rendition of *Somewhere Over the Rainbow* by Ariana Grande, however heart-felt, is not going to deliver us from the war on terror.

Sometimes the most loving thing we can do for our friends is to throw buckets of cold water over these "deliverances". They may be good, but they're not great. Marvel heroes fight each other, are proud, don't listen, aren't able to rescue everyone, and in the Marvel universe evil is still a powerful force. Or what about David Tennant's tenth "Dr Who", who is known for his catchphrase "I'm sorry, I'm so sorry" because he too couldn't rescue people. (There's a compilation clip on YouTube of him saying sorry 120 times over three series!) [55]

Even when we do experience mini-deliverances in our lives, there is still that awkward and inconvenient truth of death. It's the big full stop, the dance we can't sit out from. While our society may have become experts in ignoring and sentimentalising death, the COVID pandemic served to highlight people's fear of sickness and death. This is understandable—after all, if one believes that this life is all that there is, then the preservation of life at all costs (even at the expense of its quality) becomes the ultimate goal. Existence is everything. You could call it the idolisation of life.

So how does the gospel of Jesus Christ subversively fulfil this magnetic point of deliverance? Here are the main points of the Christian story I would want to highlight in our framework and portrait of Jesus.

The Deliverance Frame-work

Deliverance can only come with the right diagnosis. Our Creator's diagnosis is a hard one to take but it's one we must hear. The war within ourselves, between ourselves and with the spiritual and natural realms around us—the war that we long to be rescued from—has to be understood to be a symptom rather than the cause; as fruit rather than root.

Jesus himself spoke directly about what we need delivering from. It's even worse than environmental or economic ruin, or even death itself. "What's the worst that could happen?" we sometimes ask. Jesus says that it's this:

> I tell you, my friends, do not be afraid of those who kill the body and after that can do no more. But I will show you whom you should fear: fear him who, after your body has been killed, has authority to throw you into hell. Yes, I tell you, fear him.
>
> (Luke 12 v 4-5)

Jesus says that our greatest fear ought to be the prospect of standing before the one who created us, knowing that we have consistently spurned his love and chosen created things as our objects of trust and devotion, and not him. This is to be feared more than physical death. It's our broken relationship with God and the prospect of an eternity under his judgment that we need deliverance from.

The frustrations, brokenness, suffering and death from which we seek deliverance are not meaningless random events, but warning signs and miniature foretastes of the terrible eternal realities for those who remain unreconciled to God. These are ways in which the "wrath of God" is being revealed now (Romans 1 v 18) and are shadows of the wrath to come (1 Thessalonians 1 v 10). This final expression of God's judgment will be one of unbearable total separation and total loss.

And however much our culture tries to ignore, cover up, make-over and reinterpret these warning signs of suffering and death (and boy do we try hard!), deep down we know there is something wrong with it all. We grieve death and rail against it because we know *that it isn't meant to be like this.*

Jesus: The Way Out

But let me offer you Jesus:

> *Jesus said ... "I am the resurrection and the life. The one who believes in me will live, even though they die." (John 11 v 25)*

The context for this remarkable statement is actually something quite "normal", in the sense that it is something many of us have experienced or invariably will: the death of a friend. But nothing about grief feels normal. If you have experienced loss (and I have), you'll know what it does to your insides. My stomach is knotting just thinking about it again.

In John 11, Jesus' friend Lazarus has died. And Jesus is grieving. He is angry and tearful because he knows that *it isn't meant to be like this*. And unlike those around him, who only grieve over a physical death, Jesus also grieves the spiritual realities behind it—the unbelief of the world and the terrible consequences of human rebellion against God which plunges us all into death and darkness. Jesus sees it all in all its ugliness, and he rails against it.

And if you know the story, you'll know what happens next: amazingly, Jesus brings Lazarus back to life; back from the dead. Jesus tells us at the beginning of the story (and even before Lazarus has died!) that the point of this resurrection is to bring God glory. But we can also say that Jesus raises Lazarus because he loves him and his family. Jesus loves his friends.

And Jesus raises Lazarus in order to point to a deeper truth, a deeper reality about who he is and what he has come to do. The raising of Lazarus is not really about Lazarus but about Jesus. It shows that Jesus' special statement about himself is true: he really is the resurrection and the life. That statement is not just about physical life and existence, but spiritual realities. As one commentator puts it, "In the person and work of Jesus, life is no longer bound by death, and death no longer may wilfully intrude into life".[56] The certainty of death has been shattered and transformed by Jesus; this was previewed in Lazarus' resurrection and undeniably declared in Jesus' own.

Jesus confronts our cultural narratives by insisting that we cannot deliver ourselves. We cannot pull ourselves together if we just try a bit harder. We need him to save us; we need him to die for us. Jesus was delivered *over to* death so that we could be delivered *from* death. When Jesus died on the cross, he took God's wrath at our sin upon himself. Then, in his resurrection, Jesus was vindicated—the empty tomb was God's seal of approval on Christ's sacrifice on our behalf. There was nothing more to do. It was finished; sin had been dealt with. In the words of the apostle Paul, "He was *delivered* over to death for our sins and was raised to life for our justification" (Romans 4 v 25, emphasis added).

And Christ's resurrection guarantees our own resurrection in the future. In him, our greatest fear has been overcome and removed. What is more, we can enjoy true spiritual life right now. We can know and experience forgiveness. We can have our shame taken away. We can experience the joy of reconciliation with God and with others. Nothing can now separate us from the love of God that is in Christ Jesus our Lord (Romans 8 v 37-39).

Yes, Christians still face suffering and death in the present. Death is still ugly and painful, and Jesus himself in the Lord's Prayer tells us that we should pray, "Deliver us from evil" (Matthew 6 v 13, ESV). However, the fear of death is shrunk down to size as we recognise the towering authority and power of Jesus Christ's lordship over everything. Those who know Jesus Christ share in that authority with him; so much so that we can even say that death is "ours" (1 Corinthians 3 v 22). We own it! Death is no longer a penalty for sin but a stingless servant and gateway to life. As one Christian catechism (a guide to instruct in the faith) teaches:

"Q: Since then Christ died for us, why must we also die?

"A: Our death is not a satisfaction for our sin, but only a dying to sin and an entering into eternal life."

(Heidelberg Catechism Q. 42)

It's hard to articulate all this but I've experienced it profoundly as I've attended funeral services for dear friends who have died loving Jesus—and perhaps you have too. At *one and the same time* there has been deep, deep sadness and loss and also deep, deep joy and thanksgiving and hope. I miss my friends terribly but know I will see them again. Such hope is not based on me crossing my fingers but on the fact that 2,000 years ago Jesus Christ came back from the dead, and that he promised everlasting life for those who know him. For a world that is searching for deliverance from death, this is wonderfully good news.

Yet the deliverance Jesus offers also subverts our expectations, because it will mean dying to ourselves. So often the things we look to for "deliverance" are really about meeting our own desires for pleasure, comfort and safety. Jesus says: "Whoever wants to be my disciple must deny themselves and take up their cross and follow me" (Mark 8 v 34). There is no cloying sentimentality about the authentic Christian life in Jesus' words. It's often tough and hard. The kitsch Christian is a fake Christian.

But the deliverance I'm describing also exceeds our expectations. Jesus' resurrection is the breaking in of a new world order; the dawning of a new day; the firstfruits of an abundant harvest. The deliverance Jesus promises is not about escape from this world but about its restoration, not just at the personal level, but at the cosmic level.

And this isn't just for the future; it begins today. God uses us as his servants to demonstrate—albeit imperfectly—his reconciliation, peace, and justice in our lives, families and communities, here and now. He sets us free from sin *now* so that we might serve others in using all the gifts he has given us. This is a vision which has inspired and continues to motivate hundreds of thousands of Christian believers across the world to look out and reach out to those in need—the marginalized, the immigrant, the weak and the poor. As our friend J.H. Bavinck says:

"For a long time Christians have overemphasised the fact that the Christian faith is something that concerns mankind's innermost being and is the way to salvation, without paying enough attention to the fact that faith places men and women in the perspective of the kingdom. That includes the fact that the believer must strive after a new world. Something of the power of the new life in Jesus Christ must penetrate social and economic life, commerce and industry, science and art. We must not leave any sector of individual or social life to its own devices. God wants us to gather together right now all things in this world under one head, Christ." [57]

We Christians sometimes worry that focusing on these "earthly" deliverances will distract us from proclaiming the "ultimate" deliverance in Christ. But when we look back in history, we see that this needn't be so. In fact, it's when Christians have been clearest and most passionate about people's need for ultimate deliverance that they have been at the vanguard of advancing deliverances in education, in science, in justice, in welfare, in politics, in economics and in the arts. The gospel needn't squash our natural desire to make the world a better place. It doesn't diminish our drive to improve the human condition that we saw demonstrated in chapter 5. Instead, it sets these longings in a bigger story and frees our efforts from futility, because our labour in the Lord is not in vain (1 Corinthians 15 v 58).

Because, one day, Christ's deliverance will be completed and this world will be liberated and made new. Every experience we have now of resolution, reconciliation and restoration—be it as individuals or as communities—is a foretaste in a final act of deliverance where all wrongs will be righted and where all tears will be wiped away and where there will be no more death or mourning or crying or pain.

Is this wishful thinking? Well, *not if Jesus' resurrection really did happen.* As Paul said to the intelligentsia of his day:

> [God] has set a day when he will judge the world with justice by the man he has appointed. He has given proof of this to everyone by raising him from the dead. (Acts 17 v 31)

In his offer of deliverance from death to life through his own death and resurrection, Jesus shows himself to be the subversive fulfilment of the magnetic point of deliverance. So we invite others to turn around and come to him.

12. JESUS
The Way of Control

In Paul Thomas Anderson's film *The Master*, the deeply troubled and traumatized navy veteran Freddie Quell (Joaquin Phoenix) comes under the spell of Lancaster Dodd, cult leader of "The Cause" (Philip Seymour Hoffman). In one of the final scenes, Dodd challenges Freddie:

"Free winds and no tyranny for you, Freddie, sailor of the seas. You pay no rent, free to go where you please. Then go, go to that landless latitude and good luck. If you figure a way to live without serving a master, any master, then let the rest of us know, will you? For you'd be the first in the history of the world."

Is it possible to live without serving a master? Is there a way that we can control our fate? Those were the questions posed by our fourth magnetic point, destiny. The itch that we scratch and scratch until it is red raw is how we hold together—or rather, *can't* hold together—the feeling that we both lead and yet undergo our lives.

On the one hand, we *want* to be in control, and *think* we are in control, and manage and manipulate things so that we *are* in control. It's in this pursuit of control that the most disenchanted and the most enchanted join hands, as illustrated by C.S. Lewis's interesting comparison between magic and technology:

"There is something which unites magic and applied science [i.e. technology] while separating both from the 'wisdom' of earlier ages. For the wise men of old the cardinal problem had been how to conform the soul to reality, and the solution had been knowledge, self-discipline, and virtue. For magic and applied science alike the problem is how to subdue reality to the wishes of men; the solution is a technique."[58]

Although they might seem to belong in different worlds, the professor of artificial intelligence and the shaman wearing a lucky charm are actually holding hands.

However, at the same time we know that we are *not* the masters of our own destiny and that in so many ways we are controlled and captive to external forces. This could be to the housing market, our DNA, or a mysterious force that makes the phones ring in the office when someone says "Quiet". Although at one level we struggle with these masters— resenting the scripts they make us act out and the sacrifices we make for them—at another level we want and need them because they provide us with a canopy of meaning. It's ironic that the silence of not uttering "Quiet" is actually a loud cry for help in what often seems a chaotic and meaningless world. It's doubly ironic though that the supposed forces that make the phones ring aren't great conversationalists—they never seem to answer back. Indeed, you could say they are "Quiet"...

And so when it comes to destiny we often end up disappointed and disillusioned. Our teenage girl on *Wanna Be a Star?* has had her dreams shattered, but she was so sure it was "meant to be". Although she checks her mobile every day, strangely the production company never rings to ask if they can come and film her back in her normal life and she's left feeling crushed. And although in the 2020s I have access to more information than ever about my personality type, my ancestry, my ethnicity, or the oppressive regime over me, I don't feel more liberated but instead more trapped by my character, my heritage, my genes and my economic status. I'm a victim of circumstance. I feel my powers of responsibility and agency ebbing away and I am reduced to a passive and anxious state. And every time I resolve through gritted teeth that I'm going to get out of that rut, or break out of that habit, I always seem to fall back to the same old patterns, or fall into new patterns that have their own demands. Perhaps I just need to try harder, practise more, say the right words, and go through the rituals to "make it happen" or to receive "blessing". But it's tiring and I just seem to do more and more for less and less. Maybe I'm cursed...

These are the questions we wrestle with when it comes to destiny: Is there a way to be in control? Or am I under the control of something or someone else?

So how does the gospel of Jesus Christ subversively fulfil this magnetic point of destiny? Here are the main points of the Christian story to emphasise in our conversations around this subject.

The Destiny Frame-work

It will be no surprise that once again we start with the fact that we are created in God's image.[59] God has given humans a unique responsibility: to take care of creation, to shape it, work with it, and make a home out of it using the imagination and ingenuity we've been given. But we're only stewards. The owner is God. He is sovereign. Our responsibility is only a delegated one. We're to look up and know that it's God who made us, loves us, and sustains us; he's the one who gives us the blueprint to work from and the framework to work within.

However, something has gone terribly wrong. Humans wanted to be like God, and so we decided to make up our own blueprint and attempt to go it alone with our own plans. As a result, relationships that were once in harmony have now gone haywire. Dominion over creation has been replaced by domination; trust in our Creator has been replaced with overdependence on created things.

Deep down we know that we're not divine and that we need something greater than us in which to find meaning and legitimacy. So we still invest in other things that can give us that ultimate sense of meaning and purpose. Perhaps it's people—a partner, kids, family. Perhaps it's an institution or a cause. Perhaps it's the belief in fate or chance. It can be anything that finishes the sentence "I live for..." It's ironic, but in this way we create our own designer deities. Of course, it helps us that many of these substitute gods are impersonal, because then we don't have to be accountable to them as we would our true Creator. Impersonal things don't care. They can't, they're im-(meaning "not"-)personal. And if our substitute god is a person, it helps us that they are never absolute, because then we have the option of switching them for something else if they get too close and start making too many demands of us.

The problem with these alternative sources of meaning is that they don't give us the control we want. They can't provide all the answers, there are always gaps in their stories, or extra pieces that don't fit into the picture they would have us work towards. And so when these ultimate explanations don't give us the big-picture meaning and security we need, our reaction is to assert our mastery in the little things, and over things we know we can control. This might be our personal relationships, or our personal living space or simply our own bodies. Our dominion over creation becomes domination as once again we play at pretending to be like God.

The fruit of all this does not taste good. Indeed, it's rotten to the core, but we see it all around us. As one writer says:

"If we try to make something finite fill the place that only God can fill, we will try to extract an unrealistic level of meaning from that idol. When it does not work, it invites us to try harder. It should not surprise us in a deeply idolatrous society that books on co-dependency and addiction form a growth industry. People feel enslaved to substances, to unwanted behaviour, and to each other." [60]

Is it inevitable that humans continue in this vicious cycle of domination and overdependence? Will we always feel that we are both victims and oppressors at the same time—a bundle of being in control, out of control and under the control of something else?

Jesus: The One in Control

The answer to those questions is no. Let me offer you Jesus. Jesus says:

I am the good shepherd. The good shepherd lays down his life for the sheep. (John 10 v 11)

This Christian view of destiny is relational and deeply, deeply personal. Jesus calls himself the "good shepherd". The shepherd is the one who leads. Jesus is the one who calls the shots (not us). He leads, we follow. But Jesus is a good shepherd. He leads us lovingly. He knows the sheep and calls them by name (v 3, 14). We're not a seething mass of anonymous humanity to Jesus. We're individuals. And he has shown his good shepherding supremely in laying down his life for his sheep.

Time and again in the Gospels, we see how Jesus demonstrated perfect dominion over his creation in the miracles he performed. But he did so in a way that was not oppressive but loving. When the mother-in-law of his disciple Simon Peter was ill with a high temperature, Jesus called the fever out (Luke 4 v 38-39). When a man came to him with terrible leprosy, Jesus made him clean (Luke 5 v 12-16). When a centurion appealed to Jesus on behalf of his dying servant, Jesus healed him (Luke 7 v 1-10). I could go on and on... Jesus had power and authority over nature.

And once there was a man possessed by an evil spirit; a spirit that knew who Jesus was. And Jesus rebuked the demon and he came out of the man. The Gospel-writer Luke tells us that "all the people were amazed and said to each other, 'What words these are! With authority and power he gives orders to impure spirits and they come out!'" (Luke 4 v 36). Jesus had power and authority over the supernatural world.

Yet at the same time, Jesus loved and trusted his Father in heaven perfectly; so much so that he willingly went to the cross. When Jesus was captive and a victim of the political superpower of his day, he could say calmly and resolutely to his captors and oppressors, "You would have no power over me if it were not given to you from above" (John 19 v 11).

Jesus reveals that the world is not chaotic and meaningless. It is not governed by capricious finite "gods", or by a grinding impersonal fate which makes us automatons. The Bible affirms that yes, there is a sense in which we are both in control and under control—because there is both human responsibility and divine sovereignty. And while the interplay between the two is never fully explained or comprehended by our finite minds, it has been graciously revealed to us in space and time in the death of Christ. As Peter told the Jewish people in Jerusalem: "This man was handed over to you by God's deliberate plan and foreknowledge; and you, with the help of wicked men, put him to death by nailing him to the cross" (Acts 2 v 23). Yet far from needing to feel trapped by shadowy forces or a cosmic fatalism, the Christian view of destiny is liberating because we believe that our good God has an unfolding plan for our lives, and that through all the ups and downs and twists and turns, we will get to the destination he's promised. We can trust his plan because we can trust him.

As our good shepherd, Jesus' control over our lives is neither impersonal nor tyrannical. Our obedience to him is not akin to throwing our hands up and submitting to fate. Instead, we obey in the context of a relationship of love. With Jesus I don't have to choose between powerless love or loveless power. Nor do I have to choose between either loving Jesus or obeying Jesus. Rather, those who love Jesus do what he says, and those who do what Jesus says demonstrate their love for him.

We know that Lancaster Dodd in *The Master* is right: there's no way to live without serving a master. In the words of Bob Dylan, "You're gonna have to serve somebody". And when we compare Jesus' shepherding with the other shepherds around, his goodness shines even more brightly. I remember speaking to a drug addict in recovery who had come to a church event. He told me that he could never become a Christian because he didn't like authority, so he didn't want Jesus telling him what to do. He'd never realised what I gently pointed out to him: that heroin had been telling him what to do for years and that it wasn't a nice boss. It reminded me of the following "parody" of Psalm 23 which was found beside the body of a young female suicide victim in the 1970s:

*"**The Psalm of the Addict***
King Heroin is my shepherd, I shall always want.
He maketh me to lie down in the gutters.
He leadeth me beside the troubled waters.
He destroyeth my soul.
He leadeth me in the paths of wickedness for the effort's sake.
Yea, I shall walk through the valley of poverty and will fear all
evil for thou, Heroin, art with me.
Thy Needle and capsule try to comfort me.
Thou strippest the table of groceries in the presence of my
family.
Thou robbest my head of reason.
My cup of sorrow runneth over.
Surely heroin addiction shall stalk me all the days of my life
and I will dwell in the House of the Damned forever."[61]

How much better to be under the lordship of Jesus. As one of Jesus' sheep, I am not a powerless victim in the face of impersonal socio-economic systems. Nor am I the play-thing of spiritual forces and beings that I might have to placate by some magical or mystical "technique"—be that a spell, a charm or by not saying "Quiet". Christians are not those who deny the supernatural realm or the existence of superpowers, but rather those who proclaim Christ's supremacy and reign over them both. He is the Creator, and everything else (including the supernatural) is created. Our "techniques"— whether magical or technological—are futile, because they only attempt to manipulate forces within the same created order as us. Whereas in Christ we are invited to pray to and trust in a God who is both transcendent and immanent—who is of a wholly other order—and who really is in control. Stevie Wonder was right when he said "Superstition ain't the way"!

Finally, with Jesus, we don't have to fear. Rather, as we uphold Jesus as Lord we can face the world fearlessly and joyfully. We are not fearful of death because we know Jesus has overcome death. And we are not fearful of life either, regardless of the uncertainties it holds.

John Root is a Christian minister who wrote an article in the British newspaper The Times on the Liverpool Football Club manager Jürgen Klopp on the day of the 2019 Champions League final. His article begins like this:

"Jürgen Klopp, the manager of Liverpool, who play Tottenham Hotspur in the final of the Champions League tonight, has openly professed his Christian faith.

"Explaining the impact of his upbringing in a Lutheran home, he says: 'There is nothing so important to me that I cannot bear to lose it, and that is why I find I have no reason to fear. But the most important point is that this lust for life is actually connected to my faith. I am a Christian and so I see life as a gift that should be enjoyed sensibly.'

"'Gift' has the same root as 'grace', the most central word in Christian vocabulary, while other words that flow from it— such as trust, freedom, confidence, generosity and abundance— are marks of Klopp's approach to football. In the background lies Luther's central affirmation that we are made right with God solely through receiving by faith His grace towards us in Jesus Christ, expressing the paradox of St Paul's words: 'Having nothing, and possessing all things' (II Corinthians vi:10). The importance of our salvation does not obliterate the value of life

in the world, but rather sets us free to live joyfully, creatively and responsibly.

"The most seminal Lutheran of the 20th century, the pastor/ theologian Dietrich Bonhoeffer, who was executed by the Nazis in 1945, coined the distinction between the 'ultimate' (salvation in Christ) and the 'penultimate' of living under Christ in this world. In his book Ethics he writes: 'Jesus lets human reality exist as penultimate, neither making it self-sufficient nor destroying it—a penultimate that will be taken seriously and not seriously in its own way.'

"Klopp and Bonhoeffer drink from the same theological stream. Several journalists have noted Klopp's ability to regain perspective quickly after intense involvement in a match— that is, to return rapidly to recognising its 'penultimacy'. His comment after losing the Europa League final to Seville in 2016 was: 'It's not the most important thing in the world, it just feels like it.' Hours after last season's Champions League final defeat by Real Madrid he was in a bar singing with Liverpool fans.

"One result is the 'lust for life'—he laughs more than any manager in the history of the Premier League. A further result is freedom from fear, and liberating teams to play confidently, joyously and positively. Trent Alexander-Arnold's quickly taken corner that led to Liverpool's winning goal against Barcelona in their Champions League semi-final last month was the sign of a young player trusted with the freedom to improvise."[62]

Klopp shows us something of what it looks like to have a Christian sense of destiny. In Jesus Christ's sovereign control and tender care we find the subversive fulfilment of the magnetic point of destiny. So we invite others to turn around and come to him.

13. JESUS
The Way Beyond

The fifth and final magnetic point was what we called higher power. Is there *a way beyond* the material world—a way to experience transcendence? We described this point as the "Super"-magnetic point. It's where totality, norm, deliverance and destiny irresistibly lead and converge. We may be led kicking and screaming to the notion of a higher power in disenchanted denial, or we may eagerly move towards it in enchantment. However we come to it, it's behind the other points when the curtains are pulled apart. This higher power is the reality behind reality; indeed, it is our understanding of ultimate reality. But what is it? Who is it? Is it impersonal or personal? If it's personal, what are his/her/its intentions towards me? Is this higher power benign and good? Is this higher power malevolent and evil? Does it control me or can I control it, or at least influence it? How can I connect with this higher power?

The Higher Power Frame-work

I'll be disappointed if at this point in the book you're not tracking where we are heading: that's right, Jesus Christ is the subversive fulfilment of the higher power. He is *the* "big reveal". Or perhaps more appropriately, he is the revelation. As the theologian Lesslie Newbigin memorably put it, "Christ is the clue to all that is".[63] We do not worship a "thing" or an "it" but a someone—someone maximally absolute and maximally personal, who is both transcendent and immanent. We worship one who has reached down to us in grace, the Word made flesh.

As I've described the magnetic points, I've argued that they are part of our human constitution as God's created image-bearers—those who are dependent upon God and accountable to him, but who are supressing and substituting these truths. I contend these points are present in some form in all peoples, cultures and religious traditions, at all times. However, we cannot disregard the impact of both *history* and *culture*—in all their twisty-turny complexity—on the way in which the magnetic points are manifested in seemingly endless configurations. In this sense, none of us are born "box fresh". We all come from somewhere and have a history and a culture that shapes us and which these magnetic points express. When it comes to this final magnetic point, this is particularly important to remember because of the place of the Christian faith in the history and culture of the West.

Whether it lifts our hearts or makes us shake a fist, or roll our eyes, or even just shrug our shoulders, it's difficult to deny historian Jaroslav Pelikan's statement that "Jesus of Nazareth has been the dominant figure in the history of Western culture for almost twenty centuries. If it were possible, with some sort of super magnet, to pull up out of that history every scrap of metal bearing at least a trace of his name, how much would be left?"[64] Similarly it's hard to argue with Italian philosopher Roberto Esposito when he notes that "all modern and contemporary thought is …

positively and negatively determined by the relation with Christianity".[65]

Now even *as Christians* we may wrestle with how to regard this history. For some, the legacy of Christianity is a positive thing—a strengthened point of contact between the gospel and our society. It's a magnetic point turbo-boost. For others, the legacy of Christianity is a negative thing—a whole load of pre-formed assumptions that puts up barriers to authentic and vibrant faith. Rather than a turbo-boost it's more like an inoculation jab.

Whatever our take here, we need to factor in this legacy into our description of where our culture is at. Just like our discussion on whether we are disenchanted or enchanted, the terrain can be bumpy and disorientating. People may still turn to the church on high days and holidays and for life events, but we know that biblical illiteracy is rife and increasing. We can still talk about the Christian legacy within our political, judicial and legal institutions, but we know that when lots of people say they don't believe in god, we can be pretty certain that their mental image of the god they don't believe in is nothing like the God of the Bible. We can truthfully say to them that we don't believe in that god either!

As I've mentioned, there are some, indeed many, who would love to find a middle way, who want the fruit of Christianity but not the root beliefs. Alan de Botton's 2012 book *Religion for Atheists* set out "to rescue some of what is beautiful, touching and wise from all that no longer seems true".[66] But without the root, the fruit will wither and die, something that I think we are experiencing in our particular cultural moment.

Perhaps our description of champing from chapter 7 typifies where we are at: a historic place of worship to God reduced to an overnight shelter so that people can paddle around the edges of the vaguely spiritual and the transcendent. Maybe these days the best we can hope for is an "experience" of light refracted through the stained glass window of a picture of Jesus.

Let me offer you a clearer and more brilliant picture.

Jesus: The Way Beyond

You'll have noticed that our portraits of Jesus and the way he subversively fulfils each magnetic point have all been attached to one of Jesus' "I am" sayings in the Gospel of John. Just as the higher power magnetic point is where the other points lead and converge, so this final "I am" saying is a climax and conclusion to everything I've argued so far. Jesus said:

> I am the light of the world. Whoever follows me will never walk in darkness, but will have the light of life. (John 8 v 12)

With Jesus we're not left guessing as to the way beyond. There is a way beyond and Jesus came to reveal it—to light up the path—and he can do so because *he comes from a world beyond*. In Jesus, "the true light that gives light to everyone was coming into the world" (John 1 v 9). He came from God, the Father (John 1 v 14). Indeed Jesus is himself God, the Son of the Father who has sent him. While "no one has ever seen God", "the one and only Son ... has made him known" (John 1 v 18). And that's something he continues to do. Now that Jesus the Son has returned to the Father, the Father and Son send the Spirit to be the presence of God with his people (John 14 v 16).

With Jesus we're not left wondering about how to connect with God (totality). He comes to be the way that we should follow (norm). He is the one who offers true and final deliverance. He is the one who is Lord of the universe but also the serving Shepherd (destiny).

Jesus subverts our culture's usual way of thinking about higher power because we have to come to him on *his* terms. The Christian faith is exclusive. It's intensely personal, not a vague feeling. But Jesus also promises something better than our vague notions of a higher power. In contrast to uncertainly he offers truth and confidence. And rather than a little tingle in my spine from standing in a cathedral while the choir is singing, Jesus offers real *life* now and for ever.

In Jesus saying he is the light of the world, he poses two questions for us human beings to take away, reflect upon and act upon. These are the questions we will want to communicate in our witness to our non-Christian friends and neighbours.

The first is this: *are you in the light about being in the dark?*

As a parent there are few things more excruciating than rushing to your crying child in the middle of the night only to step on that stray piece of Lego, only to then stub your toe on the bedframe. Wow, that hurts! We don't like the dark because we can't see what's in front of us. We can't see the dangers, let alone avoid them.

In a similar way, there are lots of people who are living their lives in the dark. Their lives seem to be a series of "stepping on lego" or "stubbing their toe" moments. They have lots of questions with few answers. But here is the fact we need to come to terms with and that Jesus tells us: without him we are in darkness. Moreover, near the start of his Gospel, John declared something even more disturbing and frankly offensive:

This is the verdict: light has come into the world, but people loved darkness instead of light because their deeds were evil.

*Everyone who does evil hates the light, and will not come into
the light for fear that their deeds will be exposed.*

(John 3 v 19-20)

Some creatures such as moths see a light and move towards
it. Others, such as cockroaches, scurry away to hide from it.
We are the latter. Our culture may think it is enlightened, but
so many are "en-darkened". That's what we've been saying
all along in terms of the cosmic game of hide-and-seek. We
are hiding and the magnetic points are the ways in which
we hide as we suppress and substitute the truth. We're not
searching for our Creator because we don't want an up-close
and personal encounter with him. We'd rather keep things at
a comfortable arms-length distance; we want a spirituality
which is conveniently impersonal and won't make demands
or look at us too closely. We'd rather not be in the spotlight
or under the microscope. What Jesus says is that true
enlightenment means recognising that we are in the dark and
that it's painful.

Second, *are you in the dark about coming into the light?*

The good news of Christianity is that you do not have to stay
in the dark. Jesus says that anyone who follows him will never
walk in darkness but will have the light of life (John 8 v 12).
Following Jesus is more than simply recognising that he's a guy
who said some helpful stuff 2,000 years ago. It's recognising
who he is and what he has come to do. Only a few verses on
from claiming to be the light of the world, Jesus says this to
those who were questioning his identity and his authority:

*"You are from below; I am from above. You are of this world; I
am not of this world. I told you that you would die in your sins; if
you do not believe that I am he, you will indeed die in your sins."*

"Who are you?" they asked.

"Just what I have been telling you from the beginning," Jesus replied. "I have much to say in judgment of you. But he who sent me is trustworthy, and what I have heard from him I tell the world."

They did not understand that he was telling them about his Father. So Jesus said, "When you have lifted up the Son of Man, then you will know that I am he and that I do nothing on my own but speak just what the Father has taught me. The one who sent me is with me; he has not left me alone, for I always do what pleases him." Even as he spoke, many believed in him.
(John 8 v 23-30)

Jesus is "from above". He truly is the higher power, the way beyond, not of this world. But he came into this world so that people would believe in him and not die in their sins. He showed his authority by being "lifted up", a term which has the most incredible double meaning. "Lifted up" refers to Jesus being exalted—it's an indication of his authority, that he really is from another world. But "lifted up" is also referring to the fact that Jesus was lifted up on a cross—a place of punishment, humiliation and defeat. This little phrase is the most amazing example of subversive fulfilment and it's also, in the words of the commentator Edward Klink, "the heart of the Christian message: the Judge has decided to receive on himself the guilt of the defendant".[67] And for those who follow Jesus—who follow him to the cross, follow him as the way—then there is *life*. Because, as we'll know if we've ever tried to grow anything, *light brings life*. Yes, light exposes, but light gives life. Jesus is the light of the world.

So the question Jesus poses to us, and which we in turn pose to others, is this: *Do you believe in him? Do you believe he is the higher power, the one from beyond? Do you believe he is the way we connect, the way to live, the way of deliverance, and the way of control?*

It's our mission to invite others to do what many did in Jesus' day, and what millions have done throughout history and around the world since—to come out of the darkness and come into the light. *Turn around and come to him.*

14. The Magnetic People

On the 28th October, 1883, Charles Spurgeon preached a sermon at the Metropolitan Tabernacle, London, entitled "The Marvellous Magnet". His text was John 12 v 32: "And I, when I am lifted up from the earth, will draw all people to myself". Spurgeon described how, when a nail is attached to an electric magnet, the nail itself becomes magnetic. In this way you can join a second nail to the first, and a third nail to the second, and so on, until you have a whole chain of nails that are held together. Spurgeon observed:

"All the magnetism comes from the first place from which it started, and when it ceases at the fountainhead there is an end of it altogether. Indeed, Jesus Christ is the great attractive magnet, and all must begin and end with him ... More and more the kingdom grows, 'ever mighty to prevail,' but all the growing and the prevailing come out of him. So it is that Jesus works— first by himself, and then by all who are in him. May the Lord make us all magnets for himself." [68]

Notwithstanding that Spurgeon has borrowed my magnet metaphor without permission, this is a tremendously exciting vision. The magnetic person magnetises a magnetic people—

the church—and the kingdom of Jesus grows as more and more are drawn to him. If we could realise that image, it would transform not only individual lives but also families, communities, and even whole cultures.

The question now becomes this: how do we become a people who are fully magnetised? There's nothing more pathetic than the weak fridge magnet that can't even hold one piece of average child artwork to the fridge and instead slides down hopelessly onto the kitchen floor. Likewise, a weak fridge-magnet faith in ourselves or others is a very sad sight.

Moreover, what makes this question more acute is that becoming demagnetised is not the only danger. Remember, as created beings we always *have* to serve someone, and Jesus said we cannot serve two masters. *We are either being formed by Christ or are being deformed by someone else. If we are not being drawn to Christ, we are being drawn away by something else.* We're often aware, on a conscious level, of our time and attention being pulled in different directions that require constant navigation and negotiation: career, family, church, leisure and so on. But spiritually, and maybe subconsciously, we face the same problem. We're being pulled in different directions towards other priorities, other loves, other ultimates, other "gods".

That's why Paul exhorted the Christian disciples in Colossae:

So then, just as you received Christ Jesus as Lord, continue to live your lives in him, rooted and built up in him, strengthened in the faith as you were taught, and overflowing with thankfulness.

See to it that no one takes you captive through hollow and deceptive philosophy, which depends on human tradition and the elemental spiritual forces of this world rather than on Christ. (Colossians 2 v 6-8)

Receiving Jesus Christ as Lord means that by God's Spirit, we confess and live out our ultimate *dependence* upon him and our *accountability* to him. The battle we face every day of our lives is to not be pulled away and taken captive by giving our hearts to other things that we end up depending upon and feeling accountable to, *rather than on Christ*. Let's consider what being pulled away might look like, using the framework of the magnetic points.

The Pull of the Points

In terms of *totality and the way to connect*, we can be pulled back into thinking that there is no big plan for God to bring "all things together". Life seems random. Nothing seems connected. Perhaps when life is vast, overwhelming and getting on top of me, I see myself as an insignificant nothing, something on the bottom of the divine shoe, and not a precious adopted child of God with a glorious inheritance. Or perhaps something else in my life gives me a greater sense of connection and personal significance than the kingdom of God, my identity in Christ and the family of God's people. Other characters in the story, which all have vital roles, suddenly start to vie for the limelight, wanting to take centre stage. Perhaps it's my nation, a political ideology, my race, my sexuality and gender, my football club, peer group or friends. Although I can say that my identity is in Christ, it's these *other connections* which starts to order my priorities, to dominate my decisions and affections, and become the primary way I define "me".

When it comes to the *norm and the way to live*, perhaps we see God's standards as rules that constrict us for rules' sake, rather than as rules that liberate us for our good. Perhaps we start to see the norm as abstract, impersonal and legal, and so we become focused on the letter of the law rather than the Spirit who inspired it. Or perhaps we think we can love Jesus without obeying his commands. Maybe we think Jesus' teaching is on the wrong side of history. Perhaps we're constantly wracked with guilt because we know we've transgressed the norm and have lost sight of Jesus as both our standard and Saviour.

For *deliverance and the way out*, perhaps we subtly and almost imperceptibly start to think that we are delivered by our routines and our purity. Perhaps we start to focus more on fixing some area of our lives—where we live or who we're with—and lose our sense of eternal perspective. We might implicitly play down that we have been delivered from hell and the finality of death. Or perhaps we go the other way and focus so much on the deliverance from the wrath to come that we forget the implications of Christ's death and resurrection for life *now*. We forget that we are delivered in order to serve others.

In terms of *destiny and the way we control*, perhaps even as Christians we can feel like victims. God's sovereign plan for our lives feels more like that infamous fickle finger of fate rather than loving fatherly care. When this happens we can question our responsibility and accountability. We can start giving excuses for our sin: my genes made me do it, my upbringing made me do it, my circumstances made me do it, Satan made me do it, God made me do it. Perhaps we look at our mis-fortunes as precisely that—bad fortune. On that road marked with suffering (to quote the Matt Redmond song), we don't say "Blessed be your name", we say, "Maybe God's got it in for me", or "Maybe God's not in control and can't help me", or "Maybe he can, but I've got to do something first so that he will". It might be that we try to take control and manipulate the variables—the kind of logic that reasons that if I do my quiet time in the morning, I'll be assured a good day. When this happens, we lose the peace of knowing that no experience is outside of Jesus' sovereign control—that he sees all things and that he himself will right all wrongs on the day of judgment.

Finally, in terms of the *higher power and the way beyond*, we experience the culmination of all the "pulls" I've just mentioned. In our daily words, actions, habits and rituals we gradually demonstrate that there are "loves of our lives" that are higher and deeper than our love for Christ. These are the loves we go to *first* in our need to find a way to connect, a way to live, a way to be delivered and a way to control. It's not that we don't believe in Jesus; we still have *a* place for him—even a very important place—in our hearts. Rather, it's that he's been subtly subordinated and squashed and has to get in the queue. He is no longer preeminent in our lives. He is no longer Lord.

That's what it looks like to be de-magnetised. Why don't you pause here and give yourself a few minutes to reflect? Go through each of those points again and ask yourself this: *on which point am I most vulnerable to being pulled away?* It might be helpful to think about this in terms of your head (what you think), hands (what you do) and heart (what you love). Are these all in sync?

Staying Fully Magnetised

Contrast this with how it looks to be constantly drawn by the magnetic person—Jesus Christ. He is the one we love and who has captured our hearts and affections. He is our totality; our norm; our deliverance; our destiny; our higher power. He is one on whom we depend and the one to whom we are accountable. He is the one who loves us sacrificially, unconditionally and tenaciously with a love that does not let us go.

When we stick to Jesus as the true vine, we become people who enjoy deep relationships with him and with others; people who enjoy both the intimacy of being known and the significance of being part of something bigger and better. We become people who are other-person centred and who are passionate about being part of God's plan to bring everything together under the lordship of Jesus.

When we stick to Jesus as the way, the truth and the life, we become people who know that life is messy and complicated, but who know that Jesus' standards are wise, and that they offer us a solid and stable ground for human flourishing. We become people who know that Jesus is not just the standard, but the Saviour—and so experience the liberation of forgiveness, knowing our acceptance is not based on our obedience. Whenever we're struggling to see how God's norms apply, we look to the life of Christ, *the* human of humans, who loved and lived the law of God perfectly.

When we stick to Jesus as the resurrection and the life, we become people who embrace life with joy, creativity and even abandon because we know and have experienced ultimate deliverance. Although we may experience frustration, suffering and even physical death, we know that physical death is not the end but the beginning and a gateway to be with Jesus.

When we stick to Jesus as the good shepherd, we are freed from feeling weighed down, oppressed and fearful about what may or may not happen. Instead we gladly come under Jesus' authority and see the unfolding plan of our loving heavenly Father as an adventure to explore.

Finally, when we stick with Jesus as the light of the world, we become enlightened people who continue to grow "upwards" towards that light and grow "outwards" as beacons of light in a dark world.

This is what we all want to be like... but how? How do we become these kinds of fully magnetised followers of Jesus?

Of course, these changes can only happen through the power of the Holy Spirit. He is the agent of transformation. However, the Holy Spirit works through means. Here are a number of ways we stick to Jesus and Jesus sticks to us. I've put them into three overlapping categories: loving Jesus, loving our identity in Jesus and loving Jesus' body: the church.

1. Loving Jesus

In any personal relationship, we demonstrate our love by listening. After all, who wants to hang out with friends who don't listen, or agree to a second date if all the other person has done is drone on at you all evening? Love listens.

To love Jesus we must listen to him. We aren't listening so that we might gain his ear, or so that he might want to be our friend—we listen because he is himself love. And we listen to Jesus by listening to his word. As one believer put it, "I have never met Christ in the flesh. No matter, he has written me a letter. Not he, himself. He chose helpers. By his Spirit, the Spirit of truth, these helpers wrote what he wanted me to know."[69]

Our attitude to God's word is an index of our love for Jesus. In the words of the 16th century Archbishop Thomas Cranmer, "These books, therefore, ought to be much in our hands, in our eyes, in our ears, in our mouths, but most of all in our hearts".[70] It's through these words that we come alive, and it's as we continue to eat them that we remain healthy.

And yes, that means seeking to develop a daily habit of reading and listening to the Bible. Not as a tick-box exercise, but in the knowledge that as you open that book and read the pages on your lap, you hear the very words of Jesus. He is speaking, *to you*, directly. *These are the words he wants you to hear today.* Open the Bible with the same sense of expectation you would have were Jesus to come through your front door and sit on the sofa next to you. Because in a very real sense, he is. What might change if you came to God's word each day with a prayer for that kind of eagerness?

Often, we need to approach God's word a little less like I approach meal times: quickly. Although I love food, I'm a fast eater. I know one of the reasons I eat quickly is not just because I'm hungry but because I just want to get onto to the next thing. Yes, we are to "eat" God's word, but rather than wolfing it down, we need to take time to chew it over—in other words, to meditate on it. Meditation is exercising our mind upon something, mulling it over, looking at it from different angles, applying it specifically to our lives. When it comes to God's word, most of us need to be a bit less "eat to live" and a little more "live to eat". We need to spend time reflecting on the magnetic, majestic person of Jesus Christ our Lord—beholding his character, comparing it to our own, marvelling at his condescension and grace and power. It's as we spend time with Jesus that our eyes are opened to his splendour and beauty. And make no mistake: majestic meditation sits on practices of habit.

The third way we demonstrate our love for Jesus is perhaps a little less obvious. In the book of 1 Peter, the apostle writes:

Since you call on a Father who judges each person's work impartially, <u>live out your time as foreigners here in reverent</u>

fear. *For you know that it was not with perishable things such as silver or gold that you were redeemed from the empty way of life handed down to you from your ancestors, but with the precious blood of Christ, a lamb without blemish or defect.*

(1 Peter 1 v 17-19)

We love Jesus by living in reverent fear. This may seem counter-intuitive. But we need to see the way the argument flows in these verses. Peter, using the phrase "for you know", links the exhortation to live "in reverent fear" with "the precious blood of Christ". Peter is saying something like this: *You know the futility of your old life. You know the cost of liberation from that life was nothing other than the precious blood of Christ. Now in light of that: Fear! Fear living in a way that would show that the precious blood of Christ doesn't matter.* As one commentator puts it: "To continue to live in one's useless former ways is implicitly to deny the value of Christ's death".[71]

Such teaching is sobering but is the wake-up call we might need. We are so easily intoxicated by other loves and other lords. I can recall a number of occasions when I have been tempted to sin and have been wavering in that twilight zone of deliberation. But then I have remembered and prayed through this passage and it has pulled me back from the edge. Is there an area of your life where the Spirit wants to use God's word to pull you back from the edge even now? We will stay magnetised by loving Jesus, stepping into his light and allowing his glory to burn off the futility of our old life.

2. Loving Our Identity in Jesus

As we've seen throughout our description and analysis of the magnetic points, questions of identity are never far away. Who am I? What am I worth? Where do I belong? When we come to Christ in repentance and faith, we know we are given a new identity as those who are "in Christ", but the seeming chaos of the world around us means that our new identity can feel fragile and shaky. It's so easy to start feeling anxious and fearful and look for security in other things. We need an anchor. And knowing and loving our identity in Jesus will keep us magnetised to him and prevent us from being pulled away or pulled apart.

To demonstrate how our identity can anchor us, allow me to lead you on a little foray into ancient Israel. In Isaiah 41, the prophet describes a rampaging superpower that is rapidly conquering all before him and is creating great fear and trembling among the watching nations, including Israel: King Cyrus of Persia. So in verse 2 the LORD asks, *Who is behind this approaching menace?* In verse 4 the LORD gives this terrifying answer: "I am" (v 4).

The nations around Israel are blinded to what the sovereign Lord is doing behind the scenes—they can only see the approaching menace. In verses 5-7 the passage takes a darkly satirical turn as we see the trembling nations shuffle onto the stage, looking for solace and encouragement in the other, giving tepid pep talks and looking for protection from their objects of devotion.

They approach and come forward;
they help each other
and say to their companions, "Be strong!"
The metalworker encourages the goldsmith,
and the one who smooths with the hammer
spurs on the one who strikes the anvil.
One says of the welding, "It is good."
The other nails down the idol so that it will not topple.

Idols give the illusion of being an external source of help and identity. In reality, of course, they are merely the work of human hands and therefore useless in the face of threat. Idols are shaky because they are created by our shaky selves.

But Israel can look somewhere more stable for comfort to be found in the face of the approaching menace—they can look to the one *behind* the approaching menace, the Lord God who is the mastermind of history. In verses 8-10 God speaks to Israel, giving them three identities of increasing intimacy:

> *But you, Israel, my servant,*
> *Jacob, whom I have chosen,*
> *you descendants of Abraham my friend,*
> *I took you from the ends of the earth,*
> *from its farthest corners I called you.*
> *I said, "You are my servant";*
> *I have chosen you and have not rejected you.*
> *So do not fear, for I am with you;*
> *do not be dismayed, for I am your God.*
> *I will strengthen you and help you;*
> *I will uphold you with my righteous right hand.*

Israel is a servant nation, the chosen recipients of God's covenantal love (like Jacob, their forefather), and like Abraham they can even be called God's friend. Note that all of these titles only make sense in the context of there being an external source: to be servant you need a master, to be chosen you need a chooser, to be called a friend you need a friend. In their relationship to the living God, Israel has an external source of help that is for ever stable not shaky.

And the same Lord who takes hold of the hand of "little Israel" and "worm Jacob" and says "Do not fear ... I myself will help you" (v 14)—this Lord is our Lord. It is this Lord who in the first century walked out on water to meet his disciples who were struggling against the wind and waves and told them not to be afraid, because he is the great "I AM" who can control all things and who is behind all things, even the wind and the waves.

And it is in this Lord, the Lord Jesus Christ, that we are to root ourselves. As we are united to Christ by God's Spirit, we become his servants, his chosen ones, his friends. We experience the humble confidence and security in knowing who we are—in knowing we are his. So whatever life throws at us—when we're crushed by criticism, or threatened by danger, or feel like we don't belong—we can remember that we belong to Christ: treasured, safe, secure.

Over the clamouring claims of 21st-century false gods and false lords who want to pull us towards them, the Lord calls us, his "little worm" church, not to be afraid but to renew its strength. We are small, often tired, dispirited, and seemingly defeated, but our identity is stable and secure. And when we remember that, we can proclaim with increasing confidence to the scared shaky-selves all around us the magnetically attractive hope and certainty that the Lord of history offers.

3. Loving Jesus' Body: the Church

The church is one of the greatest means that God has given to magnetise us. That's why the writer of the book of Hebrews exhorts Christians to "consider how we may spur one another on towards love and good deeds, not giving up meeting together, as some are in the habit of doing, but encouraging one another—and all the more as you see the Day approaching" (Hebrews 10 v 24-25).

There are two "movements" in this wonderful symphony: our gatherings and our scatterings.

In our gatherings together, the church is the place where week by week we are recharged and re-magnetised as we come together to hear God's word and take part in the sacraments. But we do this more informally too, as we engage in the "one anotherings" that the New Testament often speaks about—loving one another, bearing with one another, building one another up. Church is not to be a "lonely crowd". As a family we do not love one another from a distance but in the mess of everyday life—when it's tough love, not easy love. And as we serve others, there is mutual magnetising going on.

Remember back in chapter 9 I shared my friend's testimony about how he was drawn to the Christian faith because of the way Lance "the fat kid" was treated? This is true for so many. A genuine, diverse, loving, trustworthy, *real* community where there is love and unity is truly magnetic. Francis Schaeffer was so right when he noted that how we relate to one another is the criterion the world uses to judge the truthfulness of our message: Christian community is the "final apologetic".[72]

When I first started teaching this material, one Christian lady told me that when she thinks of the best that the church can be, she thinks of a picture from the end of a children's book called *God's Very Good Idea* by Trillia Newbell and Catalina Echeverri (The Good Book Company, 2017). It's a picture of the noisy, joyful chaos of a church lunch with men, women and children from all kinds of ethnicities and of all ages around the table, eating, drinking and having fellowship.

Yes, God's people are a work in progress. However, the New Testament "one another" commands can't be neglected. Those outside the Christian community who are rootless, homeless, marginalised, bitter, gossiped about, and slandered, don't want to look at the church and see Christians behaving like that too. Why would they want to engage with something that's no different?

And we become re-magnetised in the more formal parts of our gatherings too. In our songs, prayers and preaching, we are reminded week by week of the beauty and appeal of the Lord Jesus. But we're also reminded of the appalling-ness of idolatry. Whether we realise it or not, our sung worship always contains a punch of the polemical. As one scholar put it: "When we sing 'Praise God from whom all blessings flow,' we are also saying 'Down with the gods from whom no blessings flow... When we sing our pretty songs of praise, it is as if we are singing 'take that you false gods (!).'"[73] I have to admit that my experience of singing in church is not like this, and I'm guessing yours isn't either—but imagine how much more we'd be magnetised by our corporate worship if we threw ourselves into it like that!

And once we are magnetised each week, we are then sent out and scattered into the world to be a magnetic presence. Let me ask you: in the places where God has called you to live your life—your home, your place of work, your places of play— what would it look like to do all things fully magnetised *by* Jesus and *for* Jesus?

As followers of the magnetic person, Jesus Christ, let us pray that we would stay magnetised by loving Jesus, loving our identity in Jesus, and loving Jesus' body, the church. Let us pray that we would be a magnetic presence in the world, demonstrating that it is Jesus Christ who answers the magnetic points that frame the lives of us all.

"May the Lord make us all magnets for himself."

Conclusion:
The Way from Here

Sometimes we're given something that we can't wait to get on and use. Maybe it's a new drill for our latest DIY project, a blender for the kitchen, a spade for the garden, or a gadget for our living room. As you come to the end of this book, I hope that you're excited about using the magnetic points. I want to encourage you and say, *have a go!* Start spotting the connection points in everyday conversation with your friends, family and neighbours. See if you can ask a question that helps people think through why they are searching in that way. Consider how you can speak of where you find that "magnetic point" satisfied fully in Jesus.

Don't expect to be able to make every connection, but start trying. Don't worry if it's a bit "clunky" and doesn't come naturally at first—it will with time. If this analysis is an accurate way of understanding how the Bible speaks about human beings, then you'll begin to see magnetic points all over the place, because the Bible is true!

And, it goes without saying, pray. Pray that God will give you opportunities. Pray that he will give you boldness. Pray that he will give you the words to say.

But please remember what I said right at the beginning of the book.

These five magnetic points are the idolatrous longings of our own hearts, not just the hearts of those around us. As you learn to identify them, understand them and apply the gospel to them, my prayer is that you'll be more excited about Jesus yourself—*and* that you'll be better equipped to share him with others. Think of your life as a flow diagram and not as a pie chart. As a pie chart, your life is divided into slices: your discipleship, your evangelism, your church, your work. All these slices are competing for our time and energy. Compare that to the Christian life as a big, connected, disciple-making flow chart, where it's all about journeying with Jesus, and where our evangelism and witness are naturally exuding from that journey.

Jesus is "the way and the truth and the life" (John 14 v 6). The "way" is not simply a door we point to, or a destination to hold out for, but it's "a way along" for all of us. So the magnetic points of totality, norm, deliverance, destiny and higher power are a helpful way to check our own hearts as we read and meditate on God's word, as we confess our sins, as we watch TV, as we socialise with our family and friends. Use them as a mental framework to work through as you prepare to teach the Bible. Moreover, use them to gently challenge other believers in their lives, pointing them always to Jesus Christ, the magnetic person.

Finally, let's help each other. Have you considered meeting up with others in your church who have read this book to chat and pray through where you've observed the magnetic points?

And why don't you tell me? I'm trying to collect lots of examples of the magnetic points that we can all share. I've set up an email address which people have been using to send me in their magnetic point examples, some of which have appeared in this book. I look forward to hearing from you: themagneticpoints@gmail.com

Appendix:
Magnetic Preaching

Then Philip opened his mouth, and began at the same scripture,
and preached unto him Jesus.
(Acts 8 v 35, KJV)

For those of us given the responsibility to teach and preach God's word, our goal, in the power of the Holy Spirit, is to offer Christ to people, both Christians and non-Christians. We want to preach Christ crucified in a way which engages all the faculties: intellect, emotion, will, imagination and so on. We want our preaching to change people's hearts, touching their ultimate hopes, fears and commitments. We strive to make our application connect with the normal everyday lives of people in all their work, rest and play. We seek to feed people, so that on full stomachs they can be sent out week by week into their God-given callings and be strengthened and sustained in their witness.

Using the magnetic points can help us to prepare those kinds of sermons. They can act as a bridge to connect our preaching to the lives of our listeners. Or to put it another way, the magnetic points can be an aide in what John Stott famously called the "double listening" of having the Bible in one hand and the newspaper (or news feed, blog or podcast) in the other.

The magnetic points are simply a way of unpacking a theological anthropology—that is, a way to articulate *how the Bible explains human beings*. We are that messy mix of seeking God and trying to escape from him. The call for God's image-bearers to turn from idols to the living God is a constant theme from Genesis to Revelation. Consequently, as preachers and teachers declare God's word from week to week, we cannot avoid touching on themes of totality, norm, deliverance, destiny and higher power.

What the magnetic points analysis does is to give an explicit name and framework to what might often be more implicit and less organised. Perennial biblical themes can be refracted through the magnetic points. Biblical characters can be described and analysed through this lens. Remember that all five magnetic points are perspectives on or "ways in" to the one religious consciousness, and all five points find their subversive fulfilment in Christ. The points can be distinguished for teaching purposes but they can't really be compartmentalised. They all impinge upon the others, all imply the others, and all lead to the magnetic person, Jesus Christ.

So, for example, a passage where we come across the common New Testament phrase "in Christ" (for example, 2 Corinthians 5 v 17; Galatians 3 v 26-28) can be expounded in terms of totality. You could use some of the examples from chapter 3 to demonstrate our universal longing for connection (or better yet, find a recent example that's relevant to your context). Then explain the implications of being "in Christ" for our communion with God and our identity, and show how this delivers an infinitely superior sense of connection than any of the other places we look.

Similarly, passages that deal with ethical instruction (for example, Colossians 3; 1 Peter 3) can be understood terms of Jesus being both the standard and the Saviour in our relationship to the norm. Jesus' miracles can be seen through the magnetic point of deliverance. Texts where we need to expound the sovereignty of God and human responsibility (for example, numerous Old Testament narratives) can be seen in the light of the magnetic point of destiny, as we show that these seemingly paradoxical doctrines actually make sense of what we observe around us.

And we can work through what idolatrous responses to these issues look like, as compared to worship of the true higher power. For example, at the heart of Psalm 92 is the little statement: "But you, LORD, are for ever exalted". We can easily pass this by as almost a "throwaway" line of praise. But as we've seen, praise in the Old Testament also implies polemic: "But you, LORD [alone and not X], are for ever exalted" (v 8). Let's name and shame what these other "higher powers" are compared to the living Lord.

Using this analysis as we prepare our preaching compels us to look closely at both how the magnetic points emerge from the biblical text we are expounding, and how they are manifesting themselves in the lives of those who sit under our teaching (both believers and unbelievers). Good questions to ask are: At a very granular level, what are the "objects of worship" of those under our care? What are their very specific and particular "takes" on totality, norm, deliverance, destiny and higher power? How does Jesus subversively fulfil this particular shape in our context? What will our applications be to make sure we are fully magnetised and not pulled away?

One word of warning, though. Note that I'm saying this analysis can be useful in our preaching and teaching *preparation*. I'm *not* saying that in every sermon we explicitly have to name a point that we're trying to hit. This would quickly become predictable and very boring. Rather, analysis like this is like scaffolding. Although scaffolding is essential to construction, who wants to look at the scaffolding? What we really want to look at is what is being built behind the scaffolding. Similarly, while it will eventually be taken down and put out of sight, the magnetic points can be extremely helpful scaffolding in our desire to construct messages that connect and confront people with the offer of Christ. It's there to help people look at him.

Acknowledgements

Thanks to all those who attended the first version of this material at Word Alive in 2019—without doubt one of my best teaching experiences ever. Thanks to those who heard later drafts given in various forms in a multitude of talks, lectures and seminars which, in the last year at least, have been delivered over Zoom in the spare bedroom. Your comments and feedback have been invaluable. Thanks to Oak Hill College for giving me the study-leave to write this all up.

As with *Plugged In*, a lot of the best cultural illustrations have not come from me but have come to me. I would particularly like to mention the following: Cori B, Mark F, Anja L, Nathan W, Amy W, Paul M, Andy W, John J, John P, Ed B, Phil A and Peter T. Thanks to Elly S and Kristi M for commenting on an early draft.

Finally, a special thanks to my editor, Rachel Jones, who once again has been just brilliant and a joy to work with.

Soli Deo Gloria.

Endnotes

1 For an account of J.H. Bavinck's life and work see eds. John Bolt, James D. Bratt & Paul J. Visser, *The J.H. Bavinck Reader* (Eerdmans, 2013), p 1-92.

2 J.H. Bavinck, "Religious Consciousness" in *The J.H. Bavinck Reader*, p 226-227.

3 Bavinck, "Religious Consciousness", p 163.

4 Quoted in Robin Thompson, *Engaging with Hindus* (The Good Book Company, 2014), p 20.

5 J.H. Bavinck, *An Introduction to the Science of Missions* (Baker Books, 1960), p 267.

6 https://twitter.com/jack/status/1071575147293769728?lang=en [accessed 21 Dec 2020].

7 Donna Tartt, *The Secret History* (Vintage, 1992), p 42.

8 Bavinck, "Religious Consciousness", p 173.

9 Rory Sutherland, "Why I'm not on board with quiet carriages", https://www.spectator.co.uk/article/why-i-m-not-on-board-with-quiet-carriages [accessed 21 Dec 2020].

10 See Aimee Farrell, "Meet Norma Normcore", https://www.vogue.co.uk/gallery/normcore-fashion-vogue-definition [accessed 21 Dec 2020].

11 Max Grobe, "From 'Seinfeld' to Steve Jobs: What was Normcore & what is it now?" https://www.highsnobiety.com/p/what-is-normcore/#:~:text=%E2%80%9CNormcore%20moves%20away%20from%20a,no%20such%20thing%20as%20normal.%E2%80%9D [accessed 21 Dec 2020].

12 https://twitter.com/daisychristo/status/1223648167385796611?lang=en [accessed 21 Dec 2020].

13 Ben Aaronovitch, *Broken Homes* (Gollancz, 2014), p 287.

14 https://www.theguardian.com/politics/2015/oct/15/boris-johnson-knocks-over-10-year-old-boy-during-rugby-game-in-japan [accessed 23 Feb 2021].

15 https://www.youtube.com/watch?v=Wvm7xymgk_k&app=desktop [accessed 21 Dec 2020].

16 https://www.cnbc.com/2020/11/07/read-joe-biden-acceptance-speech-full-text.html [accessed 21 Dec 2020].

17 https://www.theguardian.com/world/2020/may/10/boris-johnson-details-first-careful-steps-to-ease-covid-19-lockdown [accessed 21 Dec 2020].

18 "Murray Perahia talks to Tom Service", *Music Matters* 20th June 2015, available at https://www.bbc.co.uk/programmes/

b05zgf6m [accessed 21 Dec 2020].

19 https://www.hta.gov.uk/guidance-public/cryonics/definitions [accessed 21 Dec 2020].

20 https://www.reddit.com/r/cryonics/comments/g7xqml/in_an_ ama_elon_musk_on_cryonics_assuming_that_the/ [accessed 21 Dec 2020].

21 Marisa Meltzer, "How Death Got Cool", https://www. theguardian.com/news/2018/jan/12/how-death-got-cool-swedish-death-cleaning [accessed 21 Dec 2020].

22 See http://www.orderofthegooddeath.com/about.

23 Bavinck, "Religious Consciousness", p 192-193.

24 The following section is an edited version of my longer article, "Never Say 'the phones are Quiet'", *Themelios* 44/2 https://www. thegospelcoalition.org/themelios/article/never-say-the-phones-are-quiet/ [accessed 21 Dec 2020].

25 Carl Eve, "Why Police Say 'Q' not 'Quiet' and Other Eye-Openers on New Year's Eve Night Out with Officers", *Plymouth Live*, 5 January 2017, https://tinyurl.com/yylj8hmh [accessed 21 Dec 2020].

26 "Superstitious Doctors – Part I", Doc Gurley, 13 September 2007, https://tinyurl.com/y3wuq9y4. [accessed 21 Dec 2020].

27 Jonathan Lamb et al., "Does the Word 'Quiet' Really Make Things Busier? Statistics vs Superstition: Taking a Look at Medicine's 'Macbeth'", *The Bulletin of the Royal College of Surgeons of England* 99.4 (2017), p 133-36, doi:10.1308/ rcsbull.2017.133. The same reference applies to the other quotes on these pages.

28 See Stuart Vyse, "How Superstition Works", *The Atlantic*, 22 October 2013, https://www.theatlantic.com/health/ archive/2013/10/how-superstition-works/280649/ [accessed 20 Jan 2021].

29 Jonathan Liew, "No Stadium, No Transfers and Injured Players: Can Mauricio Pochettino's 'Energia Universal' Hold Out at Spurs?", *The Independent*, 23 November 2018, https://tinyurl. com/y5fo3etf [accessed 20 Jan 2021].

30 David Hytner, "Energía Universal: How Pochettino has Driven the Tottenham Revolution", The Guardian, 29 April 2017, https://tinyurl.com/y5qgwlw5 [accessed 20 Jan 2021].

31 Jonathan Haidt, *The Happiness Hypothesis: Putting Ancient Wisdom to the Test of Modern Science* (Arrow Books, 2007).

32 Bruce Hood, *The Self Illusion: Why There Is No "You" Inside Your*

Head (Constable, 2013).

33 Bavinck, "Religious Consciousness", p. 203.

34 https://www.crossway.org/articles/what-is-scientism/ [accessed 21 Dec 2020].

35 A good place to start here would be James K. A. Smith, *How (Not) to Be Secular: Reading Charles Taylor* (Eerdmans, 2014).

36 A good place to start here would be Rodney Stark, *The Triumph of Faith: Why the World is More Religious Than Ever* (Intercollegiate Studies Institute, 2015).

37 James K. A. Smith, *How (Not) to Be Secular: Reading Charles Taylor*, p 3.

38 "Understanding Unbelief: Advancing Scientific Understanding of 'Unbelief' around the World", University of Kent, https://research.kent.ac.uk/understandingunbelief/ [accessed 22 Dec 2020].

39 https://www.lancasterguardian.co.uk/news/spellbound-lancasters-new-witchcraft-shop-659668 [accessed 22 Dec 2020].

40 https://konmari.com/how-to-greet-your-home/ [accessed 22 Dec 2020].

41 https://www.penny-arcade.com/news/post/2003/06/05/vatican-city1 [accessed 22 Dec 2020].

42 https://champing.co.uk/stories/champing-in-the-media/ [accessed 22 Dec 2020].

43 Helmut Thielicke, *Man in God's World* trans. John W. Doberstein (Harper & Row, 1963), p 167. Quoted in Jeffrey L. Hamm, *Turning the Tables on Apologetics* (Pickwick Publications, 2018), p 130.

44 Bavinck, "Religious Consciousness", p 290.

45 John Calvin, *Institutes of the Christian Religion*, trans. Ford Lewis Battles (Westminster John Knox, 2006), 3.2.6.

46 Bavinck, "Religious Consciousness", p 291.

47 https://www.telegraph.co.uk/news/2019/02/24/pubs-closing-rate-one-every-12-hours-new-figures-show/ [accessed 22 Dec 2020].

48 Douglas Murray, *The Madness Of Crowds* (Bloomsbury, 2019), p 36.

49 "Seriously... Can I Still Read Harry Potter?", https://www.bbc.co.uk/sounds/play/p08y8x0s [accessed 22/12/2020].

50 William Bailey, *Defining Edges: A New Look at Picture Frames* (Harry Abrams, 2002), p 17.

51 https://www.spectator.co.uk/article/roger-scruton-an-apology-for-thinking [accessed 22/12/2020].

52 William Wilberforce, *A Practical View of Christianity*, ed. by Kevin Charles Belmonte (Hendrickson Publishers, 1996), p 198.

53 http://www.musicsaves.org/verve/interviews/10.shtml [accessed 22 Dec 2020].

54 "Murray Perahia talks to Tom Service", *Music Matters* 20th June 2015, https://www.bbc.co.uk/programmes/b05zgf6m [accessed 21/12/2020].

55 "David Tennant (The Tenth Doctor) says 'Sorry'… 120 times!", https://www.reddit.com/r/doctorwho/comments/9y5a8q/david_tennant_the_tenth_doctor_says_sorry_120/ [accessed 22 Dec 2020]

56 Edward Klink, *John* (Zondervan, 2017), p 518.

57 J.H. Bavinck, *The Church Between Temple and Mosque* (Eerdmans, 1961), p 148.

58 C. S. Lewis, *The Abolition of Man* (reprint HarperOne, 2001), p 77.

59 The first half of the analysis in this section draws on Dick Keyes, "The Idol factory", in eds. Os Guinness & John Steel, *No God But God: Breaking with the Idols of our Age* (Moody, 1992), p 29-48.

60 Keyes, "The Idol Factory", p 45.

61 Author unknown. "The Psalm of the Addict", *US Congressional Record*, July 31, 1971, vol. 117, p 28511.

62 John Root, "Credo: Why Jürgen Klopp Keeps Smiling through Triumph and Disaster", *The Times*, 1 June 2019.

63 Lesslie Newbigin, *The Gospel in a Pluralist Society* (Eerdmans, 1989), p 103.

64 Jaroslav Pelikan, *The Illustrated Jesus through the Centuries* (Yale University Press, 1997), p 114.

65 Roberto Esposito, "Flesh and Body in the Deconstruction of Christianity", *Minnesota Review* 75 (2010), p 95.

66 Alan de Botton, *Religion for Atheists* (Penguin, 2012), p 19.

67 Klink, *John*, p 412.

68 "The Marvelous Magnet" (No. 1717), Spurgeon's Sermons Vol 29: 1883, https://www.ccel.org/ccel/spurgeon/sermons29.xx.html [accessed 30 July 2019].

69 C. Van Til, "My Credo", in ed. E.R. Geehan, *Jerusalem and Athens* (P&R, 1980), p. 5.

70 Gerald Bray (ed.), *The Books of Homilies : A Critical Edition*

(James Clarke & Co., 2015), p. 8.

71 Karen Jobes, *1 Peter* (Baker, 2005), p 116.

72 Francis Schaeffer, *The Church at the End of the 20th Century* (IVP USA, 1970), p 168.

73 John D. Witvliet, "Isaiah in Christian Liturgy: Recovering Textual Contrasts and Correcting Theological Astigmatism", *Calvin Theological Journal* 39 (2004), p 135-156.

Also by Daniel Strange

Learn how to engage with everything you watch,
read and play in a positive and discerning way
that helps your relationship with Christ and
points others to him.

thegoodbook.com | thegoodbook.co.uk
thegoodbook.com.au | thegoodbook.co.nz
thegoodbook.co.in

BIBLICAL | RELEVANT | ACCESSIBLE

At The Good Book Company, we are dedicated to helping Christians and local churches grow. We believe that God's growth process always starts with hearing clearly what he has said to us through his timeless word—the Bible.

Ever since we opened our doors in 1991, we have been striving to produce Bible-based resources that bring glory to God. We have grown to become an international provider of user-friendly resources to the Christian community, with believers of all backgrounds and denominations using our books, Bible studies, devotionals, evangelistic resources, and DVD-based courses.

We want to equip ordinary Christians to live for Christ day by day, and churches to grow in their knowledge of God, their love for one another, and the effectiveness of their outreach.

Call us for a discussion of your needs or visit one of our local websites for more information on the resources and services we provide.

Your friends at The Good Book Company

thegoodbook.com | thegoodbook.co.uk
thegoodbook.com.au | thegoodbook.co.nz
thegoodbook.co.in